Postcards
from the
20ᵀᴴ century

Postcards from the 20th century

a Lifetime of memories from new zealand women

edited by
Joyce Harrison and Mavis Boyd

HarperCollins*Publishers* New Zealand

First published 1999
HarperCollins*Publishers (New Zealand) Limited*
P.O. Box 1, Auckland

Copyright © individual authors as named, 1999

The authors assert the moral right to be identified
as the authors of this work.

All rights reserved. No part of this publication may be reproduced,
stored in a retrieval system or transmitted in any form or by any means,
electronic, mechanical, photocopying, recording or otherwise, without
the prior written permission of the publishers.

ISBN 1 86950 329 5
Set in Veljovic 10.5 pt
Designed and typeset by Graeme Leather
Printed on 80 gsm Ensobelle by Griffin Press, Australia

Contents

First Word—Introduction 7

Parents & Other Ancestors 9

Childhood 33

Independence 153

Family Life 173

The Authors 201

First Word — Introduction

VISITING WORSER BAY SCHOOL ON SUNDAY MORNING

Leaning here, high over
the old tide's patient repetitions, I find myself
smiling and asking, was it forty years, truly,
or four, or—have I forgotten?—four hundred?

LAURIS EDMOND, from *Lauris Edmond Selected Poems 1975–1994*, Bridget Williams Books, 1994.

These stories, which mainly and roughly span fifty years from the 1940s forward, are real life episodes, places and people recalled from the memories of the authors. Also included are some recalled family legends dating back to the last century. Where it appeared desirable, names and places have been changed to preserve anonymity.

The authors are a diverse group of women who met as strangers, but became good friends over several years of reading their stories to each other. They have enjoyed sharing the memories that comprise this collection.

The stories are not intended to be a historical record. They have not been shaped by interviewers or social historians but are spontaneous impressions that may incidentally open a window on the social life of earlier times. Nor is this collection an anthology in the usual sense, since the stories have not been selected according to any editorial plan, apart from dividing them into blocks that mark the transition from one period of life to another—from childhood through to the time when the authors were guiding their own children. It is not surprising that most of the memories come from the most impressionable period of their lives, childhood. Within each division the randomness of the stories takes the reader down a variety of paths.

Most of the women grew up during the Depression and/or the years of World War II and its aftermath. They remember wartime anxieties and shortages, sometimes very vividly. There are moments of suspense in enemy-occupied Holland, and of tragedy, as when an East Coast Māori community learns of the death of a soldier father. The writers were not of an age, however, to be directly involved in coping with the problems of unemployment or with the 'war effort'. The New Zealand based members of the group were not, for instance, quite old enough to become landgirls or be caught up in the glamour of the Marine invasion. Their memories may be seen as among the last moments, historically, of an older order that belonged to the earlier part of the century.

Most of the pieces are short, but they are wide ranging. Some traumatic experiences, such as earthquake scares and starting boarding school, feature more than once but in different settings. The word cameos of older family characters and friends record lifestyles and attitudes that may seem unusual or quaint. Many of the stories offer glimpses of small excitements and crises, funny, or sad—or both— which have outlasted in memory the details of more notable events.

Some readers will be reminded of their own youth during those times of social upheaval and considerable change. They may find themselves recalling, as these authors have done, long forgotten people and incidents and the effect on their own later lives. Likewise they may be surprised at the power that storytelling has to strengthen a sense of family identity. For those who have grown up during the Beatles era, and into the computer age, these stories may create a clearer understanding of parents and grandparents.

Parents & Other Ancestors

1930s
Grandmothers

~

Heather Williams

Grandmother sat in state on the couch in the bay window in the drawing room, stiff and regal, looking just like the pictures of Queen Victoria—grey hair pulled severely back into a bun, hands neatly resting on a walking stick. Her frilled black, purple or brown taffeta gown began at her neck, suitably adorned with a cameo, and covered her feet. Sometimes a little lace peeked from the cuffs of her sleeves.

My sister and I always had to wait outside while Father enquired if we could come in.

Once ushered into her presence we were presented with a wrinkled cheek on which we planted a quick peck, and were then waved to sit on the long piano stool.

Grandma and Grandpa Buchanan.

Little girls were to be seen and not heard. So we sat obediently, ankles neatly crossed, hands in laps and speaking only when spoken to. After a suitable interval we were dismissed, and told we could play outside in the orchard away from the house—and not to make too much noise. If it was wet we could go to the kitchen to Aunty Violet, who would give us something to eat.

Although our grandmother seemed awfully cold and distant and never smiled, I guessed she must have loved children as my father was the youngest of thirteen, and adored her.

But oh! My other Nanna! She was all cuddly and warm and full of laughter and always busy helping others. She taught me to knit and to crochet and she had wonderful flowers in her garden. Nanna made the most delicious apple turnovers and 'water busters'. They were water biscuits made from pastry rolled paper-thin so that when they were cooked in the old wood stove and heated just right, big blisters formed, and we loved busting them.

We had a secret, my Nanna and me. She'd take me into the pantry and let me sip tea from her saucer. The sheer delight of it!

Mother wasn't a tea drinker and would have disapproved, but I suppose she might have guessed. It was a lovely secret we had, my Nanna and me.

1970s
Hinepare
~
Oho Kaa

Hinepare is one of our ancestors. She was the eldest child of a family of four and was respected in the district of Rangitukia on the East Coast. When she died, the people decided to build a special house on the marae in her memory. It is the dining hall which stands next to the meeting house. This was apt, as her husband Mataura adorns the apex of the meeting house in the form of a kōruru.

The outer walls were constructed with timber from the old schoolhouse. Wooden blocks formed the foundations. The ready-made windows, consisting of twelve tiny panes per window frame, set in threes, were also from the old schoolhouse when it was demolished. Inside the house the ceiling was lined with toetoe stalks—the neatest piece of ceiling lining I have ever seen. Every single one was the same size and length. One just cannot imagine the time, the patience, the amount of toetoe collected, and the skilled task of sizing each individual stalk, taken to complete this tremendous task. The walls were decorated with fine lattice patterns embraced by carved panels. Above the stage, depicted in the design, were her two children. The house is still there today as a sign of the love the people had for Hinepare.

Of course those people who built Hinepare in the early 40s have all passed on. The next generation did not have the same feeling for the place. Hence Hinepare over time was neglected and was in dire need of serious repairs.

Some thirty years later our family moved back to Rangitukia to be teachers at the local school. Wiremu, who was the headmaster, asked the children to write what they thought about Hinepare. The children were quite frank. They thought the building was only good for the birds; it should give up and fall down. They were ashamed of it. These stories were sent home to the parents in a school newsletter. Did that cause a stir! The phone was red-hot with calls from irate parents. A meeting was hastily called and everyone came to have their say.

From that meeting came the long and arduous journey to get Hinepare back to the once beautiful house she had been. Everyone, young and old, shared in the fundraising: social evenings with the local lads playing their hearts out, raffles, housie evenings, bring-and-buys.

Then the working bees began with Wiremu guiding them through the re-roofing, installing brand-new aluminium windows, reblocking, reflooring and then repainting the designs on the rafters. Two faithful elders took it upon themselves to be the cooks. Hinepare was once again a place to be proud of.

Just before we had a celebration for the renovated Hinepare, one of those elderly gentlemen passed away. This was considered a good omen. We knew we would achieve what we had set out to do.

When we moved to Wellington, our hearts were still with Hinepare. Dishes were still needed, and her upkeep required funds. And so in the city of Lower Hutt we ran two social evenings a year. These were quite different from the small fundraising ventures we had back at Rangitukia. The selling of the 500 tickets at $20 each was always the hardest to do. The extra-keen ones faithfully gathered at the meetings called to prepare for each social event. By the end of the meeting the tasks of hall hire and costs, the printing of tickets, the list of names of possible ticket-sellers, the band or disc jockey, the menu for supper (which included purchasing a permit for the gathering of seafood), the booking of liquor, the doorkeeper, the chief chucker-outers, were allocated to the different committee members. Wiremu, who is still the chairman, held the overall responsibility for the several social evenings we had. Today Hinepare is still being used by her descendants as she stands proud with her new ablution block and totally covered service area at the back.

We have grown older, but we still have a role in supporting what the next generation does to keep our ancestor Hinepare a place to be proud of.

1890s
Benedictus Polenaar
~
Jeannette Hunter

I never knew my grandfather, Ben Polenaar, who died the year before I was born, but I've heard so many stories of him that I feel I know him.

He was born in 1842, the only son of a head teacher of an Orthodox Jewish school in Amsterdam. He was eager to learn and did so well at school that the rich Jews of Amsterdam gave him, when he was about sixteen years old, a bursary to study in Breslau, East Germany, to become a Rabbi. Without their help he would never have been able to study—teaching didn't pay much in those days.

In the seminary he wasn't only studying the Torah; he became engrossed in the teachings of many philosophers and especially Spinoza, with the result that he lost his faith totally. The bursary was withdrawn as soon as his switch from religious studies to Ancient Languages became known. So he went, penniless, to Berlin where he studied Latin and Greek by the light of a candle in an attic, 'keeping the wolf from the door' by helping boys with their school work.

He bought, in a desperate mood, a lottery ticket and won the equivalent of $75. His father wrote: 'Now, be a bit prudent. First settle your debts, then buy yourself a warm winter coat and a decent pair of boots. Put what you've left over in bonds in a bank!'

He came back to Holland with his degree in Ancient Languages, to teach in a college, but that was a misery. He was very short, had a slight hump and was much too good-hearted and absent-minded to keep discipline in his class. At that time he saw a competition in a paper. It was a complicated puzzle, just the thing to distract him from the

Ben Polenaar (left) and a friend, Mr Hazelhof.

unpleasant realities of life, so he set about solving the puzzle, happy to exercise his unused brain once more.

He won the prize and with it came a note saying: 'You solved this problem so brilliantly that, if you're not a lawyer, you should become one'—and that's what he did.

He never became very rich, because he didn't want to press people for the money they owed him. Once he won a difficult court case for a big multinational firm, but after they got his very modest bill they decided to get a better—and more expensive—lawyer next time.

Another time he had to defend a man who had falsified paintings. The man drew my grandfather while he sat listening to his excuses. When it came to payment, the painter offered him the charcoal drawing instead of money. How lucky for us! The money would have gone long ago but the drawing is still hanging in our sitting room.

1930s
The De Soto Car
~
Mavis Boyd

The day that Dad brought home the new car I was twelve years old, and as far back as I could remember we had had a white Essex with running boards, a crank handle to start it, celluloid windows and a canvas roof. Now, in 1939, Dad suddenly appeared with a steely blue-grey De Soto, large and rectangular with a self-starter and windows which wound up and down in a delightful way. It was not a new car, being in fact ten years old, but to us it was a thing of beauty with its shiny duco and plush velvet seats.

My father had wished for a son, or preferably two, to take over the farm when he became too old. He did not realise that he would have five daughters before the boys appeared. So it came about that we grew up in a large family. At the time the 'new' car arrived my teenaged cousin from the city had come to stay.

On Sunday afternoon Dad asked, 'Who would like to come for a drive?' Needless to say, we all wanted to go and, apart from some squabbling over who would have the two coveted window seats in the rear, we settled ourselves eagerly in the car. Of course, with ten passengers, smaller children had to sit on the laps of larger ones, but we thought nothing of that. It was an aspect of life we took for granted.

All went well until we got to town, where Dad posted a letter. When he drove on again he forgot to release the handbrake. Two miles down the road we caught a whiff of burning rubber. Someone said, 'Dad, I smell smoke.'

Just at that moment we passed two young men taking their girlfriends out for a Sunday stroll. Seeing the car with ten occupants one of them called out, 'Any chance of a ride?' Above the noise of the motor, and perhaps because of the smell of smoke, this jocular cry was interpreted by us as 'Your car's on fire!' Dad slammed on the brakes, the car screeched to a halt and Dad said, 'Everyone out!'

The four doors opened and we all tumbled out with the greatest alacrity. The young people, who knew nothing about the smoke, stared in open-mouthed astonishment at this dramatic response to their request for a ride. Their stares turned to helpless mirth at what they thought was our effort to accommodate them.

When we saw their unrestrained laughter we realised that the car was not and never had been on fire. When they recovered a little they told us that it had looked as though there might be no end to the stream of children emerging from the car.

Dad explained what had happened and one of them crawled under the car to inspect the brakes and decided that no permanent damage had been done. Laughter had removed all constraint. There were a few moments of chatter with these strangers who suddenly seemed like friends one has shared a good joke with and we continued on our drive.

But the story became another of those treasured anecdotes which families share when they are together, and it always began, 'Remember the time when Dad left the handbrake on?'

1940s
The Broom Cupboard
~
Lesley Ferguson

The broom cupboard loomed tall and narrow in the confined passage and, like most broom cupboards, was kept closed to confine the pungent fumes of polishing oil that somehow dried the mouth. Besides the vacuum cleaner, broom and mop, oil and polishing rags, there were the weapons . . .

In the back corner was Pappa Hall's Boer War rifle, a German pistol captured by my father during the World War II Egyptian campaign, a lethal three-pronged fish spear from New Caledonia—a relic from the Pacific war theatre—and souvenirs such as the Indian horsetail fly swat with ivory tipped handle, and Father's swagger stick looking like a leather rod, but actually sheathing a mean slip of a dagger.

On the high shelf was an old rolled-up Union Jack, testimony of Grandfather McKenzie's school teaching days, plus elsewhere the usual stuff of broom cupboards: tennis racquets, bats, fencing foils and what have you. Any space left over certainly didn't constitute 'standing room', but even crowded broom cupboards have their emergency use . . .

Enid had completed cutting the eely-Agnes hedge and, after a shower, gathered up her dusty clothes and made a quick dash to the washhouse without bothering to cover her nakedness. Diving back through the kitchen she became aware of footsteps on the front porch tiles. Where to escape to but the nearest room, the broom cupboard?

She just managed to cram herself into it, along with the guns, brooms and odorous oily rags, as the steps entered the hall. At the other end of the passage the linen cupboard was opened. There was a pause—her heart was drumming—and then the steps retreated, the gate thudded shut—it had been the electricity meter reader.

'Thank heavens,' said Enid afterwards, 'it wasn't all bad—imagine if the meter had been in the broom cupboard!'

1800s
Ossie's Mother
~
Kay Carter

Maria was 22 when she married James. The country was Ireland and the year 1866. The daughter of an itinerant cloth merchant who lived near Belfast, Maria received a good education and taught as a pupil teacher at Tullygirvin and later qualified with a teaching diploma at an educational institute in Belfast. With this diploma she took a position at Ramelton, County Donegal, where James had his own drapery business.

James was a widower 32 years Maria's senior and popular belief handed down in the family was that Maria was the girlfriend of his eldest son. If that was so it would explain why the son shortly after emigrated to Canada, where it is said he became a 'Black Presbyterian' minister.

Maria's first three children arrived in quick succession—Joseph Campbell in 1867, Isobella in 1869, James in 1870 (sadly James died at about six weeks of age, and Isobella died in 1871). By the time the family decided to accept the opportunity offered by George Vesey Stewart's 1878 Kati Kati Settlement scheme they had six surviving children. They ranged from Joseph, then eleven, to my grandfather Oswald, who was only a few months old.

Maria's obituary in the local newspaper of 16 September 1887 reads: 'It was with a view to carrying out a plan of Lord George Hill that the Gallaher family first came to New Zealand. The intention being that they should establish in Kati Kati a depot for the Donegal Knitting Company, for the benefit of Donegal peasantry. But unfortunately the noble founder died within six months of the arrival of the family, and his scheme was not carried on by his heir.'

The ticket for the *Lady Jocelyn* cost £77 10s and the family were listed as: James, 68; Maria, 35; Joseph, 11; Maria, 7; Thomas, 5, and William and Oswald.

According to a contemporary report by a fellow passenger:

> The steamer *Shamrock* took them for a journey of an hour to the *Lady Jocelyn* lying at Carrickfergus Roads away from the scene of confusion and anxiety at the Dublin shed through torrents of rain that dampened the already low spirits of those leaving their home and friends for a long and indefinite period. Much of the tear shedding was forgotten in the confusion that existed on taking care of the bags and baggage. The scene on board was still more confusing than that left behind, with everyone looking for their luggage and trying to find out about their cabins. The ship was delayed many days as weather would not permit their departure. Due to sail on the fifteenth, it was May 20 before they weighed anchor and slowly sailed out of Belfast Lough at two o'clock in the morning.
>
> They had a pleasant voyage with a Sunday school soon established for ruddy cheeked youngsters who listened eagerly to the instructions of fair young ladies and earnest young men. A ship's newspaper was started. The general atmosphere was shocked by the grim tidings on June 5 that two cases of smallpox had broken out; Dr Ginders winning the battle, and the admiration of all, by isolating himself with the sufferers. By July 3 the Dramatic Club had produced an original play. During the voyage two children were born, one having a very brief existence on Earth.

It was August 17 when the pilot came on board at Auckland but it was another six weeks before the family continued their journey to Tauranga on the *Hinemoa* and a further six days before they reached Kati Kati.

They were disappointed to find that their allocated land was still virgin bush. No sign of the house they had expected. James was unused to the manual labour involved in clearing the land and Joseph was only a boy. It appears that at some stage a tree fell on James and he became an invalid; but not before he had occupied the land in October 1878 and erected a one-room weatherboard house with a shingled roof. The Crown Lands Ranger's report described the dwelling as measuring 30ft by 24ft, with 9ft walls, that it had a brick chimney and a value of £12. Three acres had been ploughed and 100 blue gums planted, but James

James Gallaher.   Maria Gallaher.

was not entitled to a crown grant as he had not met all the requirements for land-clearing and cultivation within the specified time.

Maria returned to teaching and became the breadwinner for the family. They moved to the teacher's house at 77 Beach Road and Maria became the head teacher, receiving in 1879 a salary of £120.

Her days were very busy for as well as teaching and caring for the older six children and an invalid husband, she continued to have a further four pregnancies. Five more sons were added to the family, four of whom survived: George Hill, Douglas Wallace, and twins Charles Canning and Henry Fletcher. As Maria taught, the older boys in her class used to take bets on how long it would be before their teacher would have to take time out from teaching to have her next baby.

On the 9th of September, 1887, at the age of 42, Maria died in Auckland of ovarian cancer, leaving a family of eight boys and one girl and her 74-year-old invalid husband.

1920s
Grandparents

~

Rachelle Calkoen

When I was small I had two grandmothers and one grandfather. Long before I was born my father's father had died and my father's mother came to live with my parents. We children didn't like her much so we didn't spend much time with her. She was always sick and spent her days in bed or sometimes in a large armchair, propped up with cushions, in front of the window. She was a real grump, but we had to go and say 'good morning' to her before we left for school or kindy.

The camphoric smell of her bedroom, mixed with the smell of old squeezed oranges, eau de cologne and other indefinable odours, is unforgettable. On her table stood a square tin, decorated with painted flowers, and another round, tallish, green tin. In the square tin were sweets, and in the green one, biscuits. When we had kissed Oma good morning we were allowed to take on one day a sweet, and the next day a biscuit, the day after a sweet again, and so on. Now I didn't like biscuits and always tried to take a sweet instead. Oma wouldn't have that at all: 'No, today is a biscuit day.'

'But Oma, I had a biscuit yesterday.'

'No, you're fibbing again,' she would say angrily. 'You had a toffee yesterday, so today you'll have a biscuit.'

She looked so fierce with her dark brown eyes and her hair all over the place, I would take a biscuit and slink out the door.

My other grandmother, whom we called Anja, was completely different, and we adored her. I loved going to her house, especially when Grandfather was still alive. He was an inventor, and it couldn't have been easy for Anja, married to a man who made all sorts of really good inventions but never patented any of them. Had he done so they would have been rich, but unfortunately he always told his friends about his inventions and how he had developed them, and they just copied them and took out the patent. His friends became quite rich, but my grandparents weren't very well off. Also, my grandfather wasn't very good at managing his money. One of the stories my mother often told about him concerned my grandparents' honeymoon in Paris. At that time Anja had very long, very beautiful thick hair. They had a lovely time in Paris, until my grandfather's money ran out—there

Oma Polenaar on her 80th birthday.

wasn't enough money for the journey back to Amsterdam! No trouble: he persuaded his poor bride to have her hair cut off, which he promptly sold so they could get home again.

Every Sunday, two of us girls would go to Anja and Grandfather's for the day. One Sunday the two big ones, Dora and Clara, and the next the two littlies, Nettie and Chel. Grandfather made all sorts of gadgets to amuse us. For instance, one day we found a 20-cm-high doll on the table in the hall. It was a laughing man (Grandfather called him Peter) with a slit in his head. Grandfather gave me a cent and told me to 'Put that in the slit.' When I did I could hear all sorts of noises inside Peter, then suddenly he opened his mouth and stuck out his tongue on which lay a round thin chocolate wrapped in silver paper. The cent could be retrieved by a little door in Peter's back. I would love to have Peter now, so that my grandchildren could play with him, but I haven't the slightest idea what happened to him.

There is a memory I have of a party—a wedding anniversary or some such—to which we were all invited and where I spent the whole day in the loo, because Grandfather had made a musical toilet roll. When the paper was pulled it sang 'Oh mein lieber Augustin, alles ist hin' (Oh my dear Augustin, everything is gone). When I had pulled all the paper off the roll I rolled it up again and it sang the song back to front. Much more amusing to a four-year-old than listening to all the talking of the aunts and uncles!

Grandfather had also made a marvellous doll's house. It had two storeys and several rooms, but the best was the bathroom, which had bath and basin, and taps with real water coming out!

He also read books to us—mostly Dickens—and although I don't think I was old enough to understand what it was all about, I loved those times. He always smoked cigars, and used the lids of the wooden cigar boxes to paint on. He painted with oils, sometimes portraits—we still have a lovely one he did of Anja—but mostly the paintings were of sailing boats and landscapes with windmills standing on the banks of rivers with a Dutch grey and cloudy sky above.

When I was playing outside I never used to take time to go to the lavatory so I often came home with wet pants. On my sixth birthday Grandfather gave me a painting, to hang in my room. It was of a little dancer, sitting on a trapeze, with a cat, a dog, a ball and an enormous parrot. It was a magic painting: every time I came home with wet pants the parrot would fly away with my painting. He always knew. However secretly I took off my pants before going to bed, the next morning my painting was gone. Luckily it came back a day later.

When Grandfather died, my mother's unmarried sister and Anja shifted to a much lighter and more modern house very near to our school. As schools in Holland finish at 12 o'clock and don't start again until 2 p.m., most children and teachers go home for lunch. As we lived a long way from the school we often went to Anja's place.

My belief in the integrity of grown-ups took a bashing when I was about ten years old. In our house the dining room was in the basement, two storeys lower than the sitting room. Oma's rooms were on the same level as the sitting room, as was my parents' bedroom. On this occasion Mother had been angry with me and I was in a huff. When it was time to eat and everybody went down to the dining room, I hid behind the piano. When they were all gone I came out, but heard a noise in the hall. Peeping around the door I saw Oma, who, as you have learned, was always in bed, or, if she came out, would shuffle from bed to chair bent over and leaning on her stick. Well . . . I saw this poor old lady running from her room to the sitting room! As I disappeared behind the piano again I saw her hasten to Mother's cupboard, take a handful of chocolates and run to her room again. Mother often chided us for taking the chocolates or biscuits, bought for visitors, from this cupboard (which we sometimes did) but I now knew that we were not the only ones. This knowledge, and the fact that Oma was only pretending to be sick, upset me for days, until I finally talked it over with Mother, only to discover, to my great surprise, that she knew all about it!

1920s
Father
~
Jeannette Hunter

'Not so hard, not so high!' I scream and laugh at the same time. An intense feeling of anticipation grips my tummy.

These are the first memories I have of my father. He is lying back on the settee and I'm sitting on his knees and we are playing my favourite game. Every time I press a button on his waistcoat he makes a certain kind of movement.

Push . . . I fly sideways, because one leg went up while the other flattened out . . . Push . . . I'm grabbed in a bear hug . . . Push . . . I fall backwards between his legs . . . Push . . . I shake up and down for quite a while.

Both my father and I have to remember which button results in what action when pressed. A sort of predecessor of a robot!

At night when Chel and I are tucked up in bed, he comes to say goodnight with his after-dinner cigar in his hand. He turns off the light and then comes to the part we're both waiting for: the glowing end of his cigar makes squiggles and loops, dots and stars in the darkness.

'Make a C, make an N,' we beg, or it might be a 'D' for my eldest sister Dora or the whole word 'Mother'. The cigar smell lingers on long after he has gone downstairs again.

Sometimes he tells us the true story of how, when he was a little boy, he fell in a bath full of water with his best clothes on—just before he was going to a party. All because his sisters dared him to walk around the rim of the bath. Or perhaps he will tell the one about everybody calling him 'the fighting gumboot', because he was always in fights and must have worn gumboots very often.

The Polenaar family.

The story I liked best was the one where Dora, when she was small, played hairdresser. She brushed his hair and put a blue ribbon around a tuft of his hair right on top of his head. Later, completely forgetting the ribbon, he put his hat on and jumped on his bicycle to arrive at his office just like the rubber doll we had with its pointed hairdo.

My father loved music but didn't play any instrument. His piano lessons were discontinued because he preferred to play a tune with his toes while sitting on top of the piano.

Later, when people started to have radios and gramophones, Father refused to have one because he didn't like 'music in a can', but instead he often took us to concerts for which I'm still thankful. He passed on his love of music to all his daughters—and, unfortunately, his inability to adequately play any instrument.

What he didn't pass on was his drawing ability. We especially liked his composite animals like a 'cabbit' or an 'elerafdary', and we puzzled over which animals had gone into the making of these creatures. (The last one had the trunk of an elephant, the neck of a giraffe, and the body of a dromedary.)

Very much later he delighted his grandchildren by drawing these fantasy animals for them when he came camping with us.

1950s
Taking It on the Chin
~
Lesley Ferguson

Although Mother's talents as an essayist, sportswoman, cook and friend were recognised and valued, she would be the first to admit that she had no mechanical ability. As for the basics of dressmaking, that involved unpicking, anxiety and swearing. Despite these tensions an immaculate garment would emerge—such as a school blouse, with unique front panels, made from joining and recutting two of the extra four raglan sleeves she had cut.

Mother's mechanical understanding was only occasionally stretched, even when her husband was away at the war. My brother John, very handy at repairing and fixing, became the man of the house.

Dad returned from the war and brought with him a small Zeiss Icon camera, taken from a captured German officer. It took minute but sharp photos and required some technical ability to use. My brother commandeered his grandfather's old Kodak 116, but Mother wanted her own camera, yearning to choose her own subjects to photograph. One day Aunty Mavis, owner of some sophisticated cameras, passed to Mother a small, square and foolproof box Brownie camera.

That same year Mother and Dad returned to Lake Waikaremoana for their camping holiday.

'This time I'll bring back the photos,' said Mother enthusiastically.

When they returned they enthused about the beauty of the trees, the bush, the lake, the remoteness, and the tortuous road they had had to navigate.

'You'll see when I get the photos,' said Mother.

When they did come back she looked through the prints and, having done so, gathered herself and the prints together and said that she would like to show us the record of her memorable trip to Waikaremoana. She passed the prints out one at a time and recited:

'The first one is taken along the road beside the lake showing how winding it is . . . '

'This is our camp . . . '

'This is one of the hotel . . . '

And so she relived her trip, passing out the prints. By the time the twelfth print came along we had seen a set of blurry images, nearly identical, but looking a bit like an image of a chin and a nose snapped from below. We were helpless with laughter, not just at the terrible photos, but at Mother's ability to make a joke of it.

'How could I do it?' she lamented. But anyone with a passing acquaintance with a box Brownie would know that the lens and the viewfinder look much the same, and if this simple device is inverted mistakes do happen—but Mother took it on the chin!

1940s
My Pāpā Koroua
~
Oho Kaa

I love my Pāpā Koroua: he speaks so softly—even when he growls.

He walks so slowly, he is never in a hurry. I love to follow him because my little feet can keep up with him. Whenever I fall and hurt myself, he sits me on his knee to care for me.

That was when I was four.

Then off to school I go—each and every day. Some days are good and some days are bad. But at the end of every day who should be there to welcome me with open arms? My Pāpā Koroua, my Pāpā Koroua.

That was when I was five.

My Pāpā loves to potter round the house, painting, repairing, always busy. The kumara and the potato patch are his pride and joy. Up with the birds before the sun he is gently pushing his hoe. Never a weed to be seen. He has hens, a few sheep and a cow as well. Never do we want for food.

At night when all the chores are done Pāpā wants a game of cards. He calls us all to sit around as he sorts out the cards. 'Nines up,' he says—shuffling the cards with glee. 'You be my partner, John,' he says to the youngest every time. John drops his eyes, he knows that Pāpā will expect him to have all the cards required for them to win. Pāpā always loves to win.

Euchre is Pāpā's game and do or die he just has to win. No matter what the score, the joker wins the game for him. He sits on it till the very last then down it comes to declare the game. When he does not get the joker, woe betide my brother John. He is reduced to tears—he is expected to win the game for them, joker or no joker.

Then I go to boarding school. I am fourteen now. That morning I leave—Pāpā is still asleep. A letter comes for me one day to say my Pāpā is very sick. He is asking for you, my mum says. She tells him I have gone to school, then he simply says, 'She didn't say goodbye.' Two weeks later my Pāpā dies. Oh how I wish I'd said goodbye.

I beg the nuns to let me go but 'No,' they say, 'Too expensive. And rules are rules—you must wait till June.' That is almost three months away. I cry and cry myself to sleep. I cross off each day on my calendar. It seems such a long, long time. In the month of May, my mum comes down to visit me. Oh, the joy! My happiness knows no bounds.

Back home in June I look around—the house, the garden, the hens are there. My Pāpā's room is still the same—the open fireplace, with a string line across it, the hook on the fireside panel that once held his corn cob back scratcher, his huge iron bed that fills the room. The photo of our great-grandfather still hangs on the wall.

Then I walk across the river to the family plot. There is Pāpā next to Nanny. Bright flowers from the garden sit so lovingly.

'Pāpā, I have come to say goodbye,' I say quietly as I sit upon his grave. 'I know I didn't say goodbye before, but how would I know that you would die? I do miss you, so very much. I do love you, Pāpā, and maybe one day I will sit on your knee again. Goodbye, goodbye.'

1800s
Links

~

Kay Carter

History was such a bore at school. I was not even remotely interested in what went on in France or the United States, or in anything about British royal history—King whoever-it-was, who had so many wives! Although I have to confess to still having a collection of books on the royal family gathered during the 1940s and '50s—particularly the stories of the young princesses.

Now history has taken on an entirely new meaning, or at least that part of history that is mine, the history of my predecessors. I am engrossed. What was life like in Scotland between 1805 and 1865? How would a man have coped in 1812 when he lost his wife, six days after the birth of their eleventh child? What did it mean, in the memento of her death, when it said: 'She enjoyed her matrimonial connection for nineteen years'? It probably means something else to us in the idiom of this century. Who brought up the children after her death? The five girls in the family emigrated to New Zealand between 1842 and 1863, three with their husbands and the other two with a sister, her husband and family. The sons all stayed behind in Scotland.

I am fascinated, contemplating what life would have been like on an emigrant ship in 1856. What was Auckland like when they arrived and what sort of life did my great-grandmother face when, after only three years in the new colony, her husband was drowned? His body was found by 'the natives' on a beach at Waiheke Island. They buried him in the sand and went over to Auckland to tell the police who came back with them a week later to dig him up and bring him back for his daughter and son-in-law to identify. Reading the coroner's report I am gripped by this real story of people who are part of my history.

Within five years the family moved to the Waikato where the sons had been granted land as payment for their services in the Land Wars. Like many others who had come from Scotland at that time, they knew and loved the land, but their chances of buying a farm were slender.

I have also discovered the accessibility of my history. I make regular visits to the National Archives, the National Library and Alexander Turnbull Library, the Cambridge Museum, Hamilton Library, Auckland City Library, Auckland Museum and many other research places—usually with a list of questions for which I need answers. Sometimes I get them, other times I find some related items, but it is so easy to be distracted that I have to be strict with myself and my time.

I have written many letters to people all over the world. I have written to people researching the same names, of the same period and place. I have made contact with previously unknown family members through Radio Pacific's 'Open Country' programme. The first time I rang the programme I was looking for a person who had written to the Cambridge Museum in 1987 quoting her grandmother's memoirs. I knew there was a connection but had no idea where she fitted in and I could not find her in phone books or electoral rolls. Within three hours of making that call I was speaking to her and arranging to spend time at Easter with her and her mother. Both were family historians. What a bonus!

Flushed with that success I decided to try again. After giving only a brief outline of the turn-of-the-century couple I was researching, I received four phone calls from descendants before lunch.

The Internet opens up other sources of information. Our names, and those of the family names we are researching, have been added to a master list for Scottish research. Replies from Glasgow University gave us access to their library catalogue. Edinburgh University replied, too, and recently photocopies arrived of the preface to a book featuring one James Muir whom I was seeking, his obituary from *Nature* magazine, a death notice from the *Glasgow Herald* and a page from *Who Was Who 1945–1950* and, for a friend who is researching Glasgow in the same early period that I am, pages about the Glasgow Fair.

So history has taken on a whole new meaning. It has become a new and vital interest as I realise special places and times to which I can now relate. The Crimean War, the potato famine in Ireland, the Highland clearances and the life, around 1790–1850, of a Scottish coalmining family in Ayrshire: all are links in a chain of which I am a part.

1800s
Bolton Street Ghost
~
Lesley Ferguson

HOTEL HAS NO PLANS TO GIVE UP ITS GHOST
So ran the the four-column headline in the *Evening Post* of 23 February, 1991, along with the following story:

> A ghost has checked into the James Cook Hotel and his booking seems to be indefinite. About four times during the past decade the ghost, described as a gentleman in a plaid coat but with an indistinct face, has woken the guests of three seventh-floor rooms.
>
> Public relations manager Peter Sayers says guests have been woken 'in the dead of night' with a cold sensation.
>
> As soon as they become aware of the apparition, it fades away, leaving behind the same sense of eerie coldness.
>
> At first hotel staff took the claims with a grain of salt, but they have become intrigued as the stories match up. Mr Sayers attributes the appearance of the ethereal gentleman to the ripping up of the nearby Bolton Street cemetery to make way for the motorway.
>
> General manager Kim Kenny said the ghost was welcome to stay . . .

Of course the ghost must be that of our great-great-grandfather William Lyon, looking for his place of peace, his grave, which had been disinterred when the new motorway was started in 1967. One and a half hectares of land was taken for the motorway, and nearly four thousand graves were disinterred and reburied in a mass grave under the Early Settlers Memorial Lawn. Surveyors surveyed, engineers engineered, tractors and trucks moved through this serene corner, and the earth crumbled. Cousin Madge Lyon reported to us that William Lyon's gravestone was collected, along with others, by the Friends of the Bolton Street Cemetery and stored in the basement of the Town Hall.

The rest of the picturesque cemetery, with its beautiful harbour views, tree-dappled shade, old monuments, moss and lichen and lovely little chapel, was declared a historic site.

More recent motorway developments had affected the cemetery about the time of the ghostly visits. Was it possible that William Lyon, thus disturbed, was seeking his abode, moving lost between his Terrace home, his Lambton Quay business, and Bolton Street?

William Lyon arrived in New Zealand in January 1840 on the *Duke of Roxburgh*. He came from Hamilton, Scotland, where he was a printer and bookseller. He set up business on Lambton Quay, at Lyon & Blair, later to become Whitcombe & Tombs. Political affairs interested him, and he became active in a newspaper of the day, the *Spectator*.

William Lyon's granddaughters, my grandmother and her sister, must have lived with their Lyon grandparents for some time. They never mentioned that their father had disappeared, leaving Maggie Kenny (née Lyon) and her two young daughters on their own.

Beatrice and Ida Kenny would tell us about swinging on the gate of their grandfather's house in Boulcott Street and running to meet him as he walked home with Sir George Grey. Later he lived on The Terrace, at 'The Den', identified with a shiny brass plate on the wrought iron gate.

At an earlier stage of his life in New Zealand he lived on a farm (at Petone?) called Glen Lyon, where it is recorded that he celebrated New Year's Eve, 1841, by ceremoniously sowing Scotch thistle. As a printer he knew his business, but as a farmer . . . ? No wonder his soul was uneasy.

It is one of those strange coincidences that the name of the James Cook manager was Kenny. One could wonder or speculate . . .

William Lyon's plot is now just opposite the seat at the top of the Denis McGrath Bridge in the Bolton Street Cemetery.

1930s
Flowers
~
Jeannette Hunter

If you could see my garden now you would think that I don't care about flowers, but you would be quite wrong. I enjoy flowers very much, I've always liked flowers, our whole family loved flowers. When I think of the two houses in Amsterdam where we lived when we were children, I see vases of flowers everywhere. My mother grew pansies in boxes we had specially made to hang over the balcony railing—something which at that time wasn't as common as it is today.

If, as children, we were very good we were allowed, as a special treat, to cut a few flowers to put in a little vase in our own room. We didn't live upstairs, on the first or second floor, as many of our friends did. We occupied a whole house—we needed it, to accommodate our big family: Father and Mother, four girls, my grandmother, two maids and—when we were very young—a nanny. We were lucky enough to have a garden at the back of our house.

My father loved gardening, much to the annoyance of the gardener, who came once every week, and pulled out everything my father had planted in 'the wrong places'. The manufacturers of scissors were very happy with my father's efforts, because he kept on losing his little cigar-snipping scissors that he carried in his waistcoat pocket. He told us—always with a bit of a sheepish grin—that he had 'planted' his scissors again, but they never grew into a scissor tree!

Flowers are very much part of everyday life in Holland. You give beautiful bouquets for special occasions, or you bring a small bunch when you go to visit friends. They are easy to buy and very cheap. Flower shops are everywhere, you can find permanent stalls on many corners of streets or on bridges over canals. Then there are the colourful flower markets, those feasts for nose and eye, and when we were young there were handcarts pushed along the street or standing in convenient spots where people could easily get at them.

I remember one lovely spring morning, late in April, when my older sisters sent me to a shop to buy some flowers for our parents' wedding anniversary. I must have been about eleven years old. Skipping along the road, the money in my clenched fist, I saw suddenly a cart absolutely laden with daffodils, brilliantly yellow like the sun itself. I couldn't resist them. The man asked me how many I wanted. Difficult decision. So he asked me how much money I had. I showed him my open fist. Then he gave me a big bunch in my arms, two bunches, three and more and more . . . I staggered home with my load, very pleased with myself. What would my sisters say when they saw how much I had got for their money?

Well, my sisters were furious—'Why didn't you buy only two bunches and bring the rest of the money back, you little idiot?'

I can't remember how my parents reacted when they saw this yellow sea of flowers greeting them in the room, but I thought it looked beautiful when we had put them in all the vases we could find, and in pots and jars and buckets.

Father bought flowers for my mother every Sunday afternoon, at a cart nearby—her favourites were freesias but, of course, they were only available in spring. One day the vendor said: 'You buy flowers from me every week. Why don't you get a subscription? It is much cheaper and you will get the flowers delivered at home.' That was a good idea, saving money and time.

Not long afterwards my parents went to buy flowers before going to a dinner party. This time it was the wife of the flower seller who stood behind the cart. 'Can I have those anemones please?' asked my father.

'No, don't take those, they are not so fresh anymore.'

'These roses?'

'No—'

'Those lilies?'

'No.'

'The lilacs?'

Every time the same reply.

At last he bought some flowers that were apparently fresh.

Before going away my father asked, puzzled: 'Tell me, what do you do with those flowers you didn't want to sell to me?'

'Oh, they go in the subscriptions!'

'If that is so, will you please cancel mine,' was all my father had to say.

Childhood

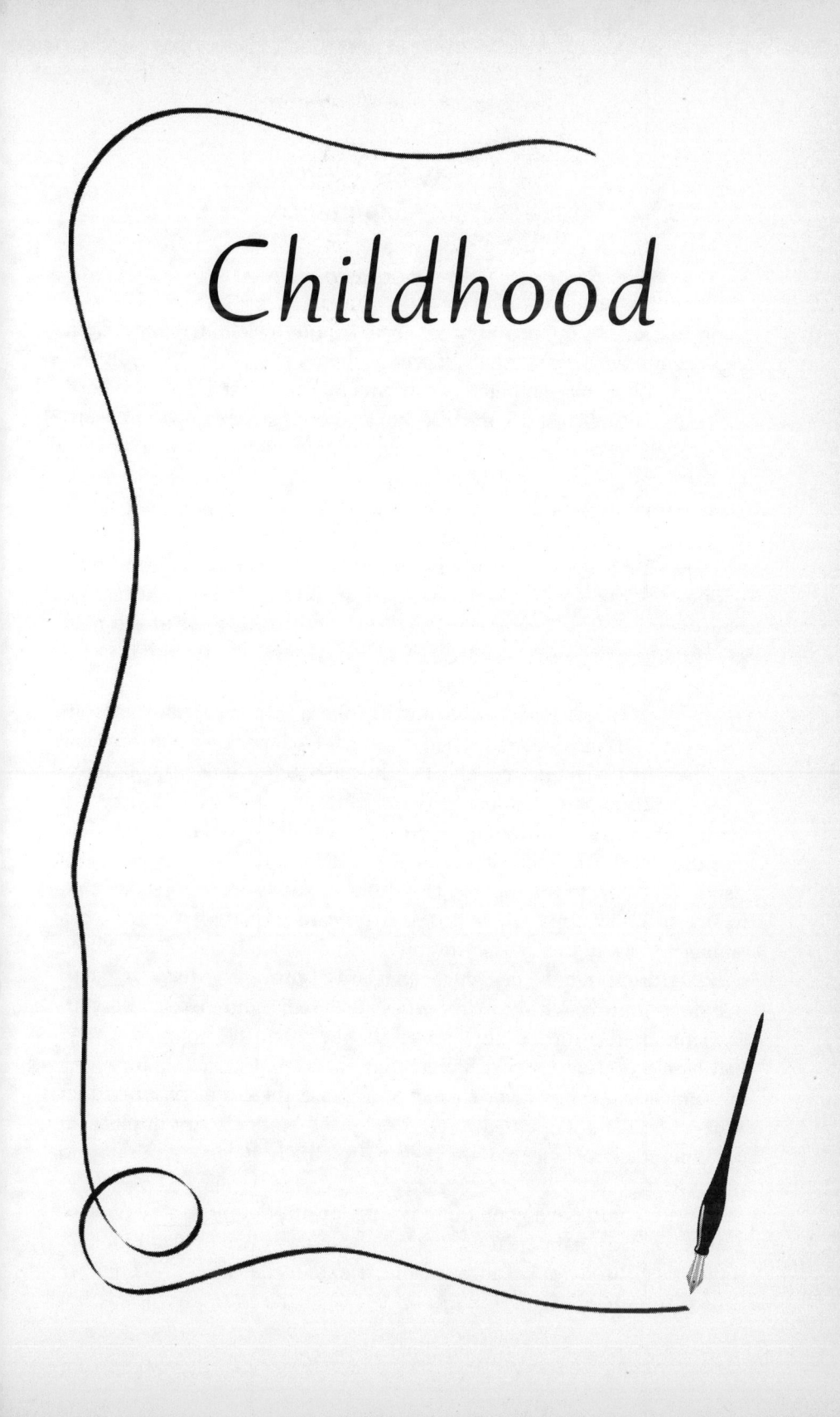

1940s
A Wartime Experience
~
Rachelle Calkoen

When Ina, one of my dearest and oldest friends, celebrated her fiftieth wedding anniversary in America where she and Jaap live, I couldn't be there to celebrate with them. But she sent me photos and copies of all the speeches, poems and so on that were given by their friends, children and by themselves on this occasion.

It is quite incomprehensible, but those two met during the war in a concentration camp. That in itself is not so incomprehensible, but that they both survived is a real miracle! Her letter triggered me off to write about the pain and fear of those war years and other miracles.

Before World War II, there were 140,000 Jews in Holland. In our small country—Holland is not much bigger than Canterbury—the Dutch managed to hide 24,000 Jews. Unfortunately, many of those were eventually found, like the family of Anne Frank (they were discovered in 1944, only a few months before the Liberation). But 18,000 survived and my parents, my sisters and I were among the lucky ones. My sister Clara's husband wasn't so lucky. In 1942 he threw a letter out of the train that was taking him away to a concentration camp, saying: 'Don't worry, I'll be back!' but that was the last she ever heard of him. After the war, when people came back from German, Polish and even Russian extermination camps, Clara showed them photos and inquired if they had seen him. Nobody ever had. When, years later, she fell in love with an Englishman, they couldn't marry because there was no proof that Albert had died. They had to go through all sorts of very unpleasant bureaucratic processes before they were finally given permission to marry.

Things could have gone quite wrong for our family as well, but for a miracle that happened in 1942. It was the 11th of September. I remember the date, because an old friend of the family, whom we called Aunt Mie, was living in our house at the time and it was her birthday. For weeks she had saved her flour coupons so that she could buy a special treat for us all on the 11th. She managed to buy six *gemberbolussen*, a ginger cake in the shape of a tennis ball and extremely succulent and yummy!

Jews weren't allowed out after 8 o'clock at night and Gentiles weren't allowed to visit Jewish people, so when at about 8.30 p.m. there was loud ringing and banging on our door we knew that it would be the German Polizei. Father quickly looked out of one of the sitting room windows and withdrew immediately when he saw the black maria standing in the street below.

Our house was built in the eighteenth century or maybe in the beginning of the nineteenth and was extremely solid: the front door was made of inches-thick oak, the house itself of big bricks and stone slabs.

'If we pretend not to be home,' said my father, 'they'll never get in.'

We had heard that there would be raids that night in the Jewish quarters. Hans Veersheym, a friend of mine whose parents lived there, had asked if her Mum and Dad and her two brothers could sleep that night in our house, as that was outside the danger zone. She didn't need to come as she was a nurse, on night duty. We also had quite a few other people living in our house, so everybody got warned to stay away from the windows and hide as best they could. We hadn't counted on our neighbours, who turned out to be collaborators and who showed the Germans how to climb from the shed in their back garden onto the shed in our back garden and into the window of my father's waiting room, on the first floor.

With their big boots they clunked over the marble floor of the hall where father's offices were and then on to the wide wooden steps of the staircase. I looked over the banister, down the round hole of the circular staircase and saw them in their black uniforms coming up. I didn't even think. I jumped in the cupboard and pulled the door shut. (Each storey had a large cupboard at the wall side of the stairs.)

The Germans were furious that we hadn't opened the door and barked to Mum and Dad that everybody in the house should put warm clothes on and pack a little suitcase and 'Hurry! Hurry! Quick! Quick!' Nettie went to the top floor to pack her suitcase. In the meantime the Germans walked in and out of all the rooms looking for more people and found in the attic the four Veersheyms who were hiding in some cupboards that were in the olden days used as beds for the servants. After a few moments it was again: 'Hurry! Hurry! Hurry!' My mother came to the stairs and stood in front of my cupboard, calling, 'Net and Chel, come quick, we'll have to go.' I didn't know if there were any Germans nearby, but I had to chance it and opened the door a crack and whispered to Mother: 'I'm not coming.' Net, Aunt Mie and all the Veersheyms came down, accompanied by several Polizei.

Mrs Fuchs and the children, Mother and Max, all with backpacks and suitcases, went down to the main entrance, but my father had refused to pack anything. He was carrying the cardboard box with Auntie's *gemberbolussen* and had put two packs of playing cards in his pockets. He refused to think that this meant concentration camp.

I don't know how long I stayed huddled in that cupboard, but when I eventually thought it was safe to come out, my legs wouldn't carry me. I sank down, shivering and shaking, and couldn't even make a plan. I knew that I would most probably never come back to our house again. I should, of course, have looked to see if there was any of my mother's jewellery left or other valuable things that I perhaps could sell, because I would certainly need some money. What did I take with me? A toothbrush, a photo album and a little vase.

I wasn't sure if the Germans had left a guard in front of the door, so I stood listening for quite a while before I dared to open the door and leave the house. I wasn't sure of the neighbours either: were they keeping an eye on our house? When it was already quite dark outside, I finally opened the door, with my heart in my throat and my legs still trembling. Nobody. Good. I went two houses along, to neighbours whom I knew I could trust, and from there I rang Wouter, a friend from my schooldays. He came immediately on his bike and transported me on the carrier to his parents' place. From there on everything is quite hazy, except that his parents were lovely and caring and put me to bed with a hot-water bottle.

The next day Wouter biked back to our house to see how things stood: if there was a possibility to rescue some of our belongings or if—as was the practice with Jewish houses—the doors would be sealed up until they had time to put everything in big removal vans. Later the contents would be placed in railway wagons and sent to Germany with big banners on the outside of the train on which was written: GIFTS FROM THE GRATEFUL INHABITANTS OF HOLLAND.

Wouter was quickly back, his face aglow with pleasure: my whole family was home again.

When they arrived at the German headquarters, everybody was chased out of the marias and into the building (formerly a secondary school) where they had to show their papers. All doctors, dentists, nurses or doctor's or dentist's assistants were exempt from deportation. There were also other reasons for exemptions, but since they changed the rules every day you could never be sure that the stamp on your identity card would keep you safe.

On Nettie's papers was written that she was a dentist's assistant and that was the reason why she was put in row A and could stay in Amsterdam. The people who were directed to row B were the unlucky ones who would be sent to a concentration camp. Nettie, Aunt Mie, Mrs Fuchs and her little ones were all in Row A but my father and mother, Max and the Veersheyms ended up in row B. And then the miracle happened!

A high-ranking German officer marched in and said: 'Ach, Herr Doktor Polenaar, what are you doing in this row? Wait a minute, there must be a mistake.'

He went over to the people who had made this decision and convinced them that Father and Mother belonged in row A. And while their row was already moving towards the waiting cattle-trucks, Father and Mother were plucked out of it! Why? Because four years earlier Father had won a case for this officer; it had been a difficult and quite important case for that man. Luckily he had just come to the headquarters and had recognised Father. If that German had not been so grateful, we probably would never have seen our parents again. We never heard or saw anything more from the two Veersheym boys (twelve and fourteen years old) and their parents, or Max.

The curfew lasted until 6 a.m., so row A was led to a house nearby, where they could wait till they were allowed to be seen on the streets again. That's when my father opened the box of *gemberbolussen*. Nobody enjoyed them much but it was good that he had the packs of cards, to shorten the hours of waiting with a few games of bridge.

My mother had had such an emotional shock that even when she was at home and out of danger, she was sick and stayed in bed for at least a week. During that time we tried to convince Father and Mother that they should 'dive under' (that's what we said when we meant 'go into hiding'). But Father wouldn't hear of it until months later, when they had again to go to the slaughter with their little suitcase. They escaped and finally decided that it was time to disappear.

1920s
Winter 1927
~
Jeannette Hunter

Today is a good day to start. Dora and Clara have done it already for at least a week, but I have been trying to get out of it. My chilblains do not like cold weather, my 'dead fingers' do not like cold weather, I *hate* cold weather, especially if it is raining and the wind is blowing mist in my face. But today the weather is clear, the sun shines and sparkles on the snow and there is no wind to speak of. So Jeanne-Laure, our Swiss nanny, dresses me up in my warmest clothes, woolly hat, thick socks and warm gloves and off we go.

My wooden skates dangle on their orange, green, yellow and white bands over my shoulders, one in front and one behind. I can feel its rounded front-knob knocking lightly against my back with every step.

The canals in the city are crowded but we are going to one at the edge of Amsterdam where there will be fewer people, we hope. When we arrive, Jeanne-Laure takes off her shoes and puts on her skating boots. She tries a few squiggles on the ice and with a flourish she is back to bind my skates with their coloured bands crosswise over my boots. My first skating lesson is about to start.

Jeanne-Laure takes my hands, crossed over in front of me, and we glide with a 'one left, one right' to the middle of the frozen canal, where she says, 'Try to get to the side.' That is the end of the lesson, and away she skates in graceful easy curves. Totally abandoned I stand on wobbly legs with people flying past to the right and left. I don't dare move. Now and then somebody uses me as a stop by grabbing me around the waist and swinging around with me, with a crunching braking sound, to glide off again.

How long I stand there, petrified, I'm not sure; it feels like hours. Then, like a warm scarf wrapped around me, a voice says: 'Do you want me to help you?' A big boy takes my hand firmly and—hoopla—we're really skating, like everybody around us. Up and down from one bridge to the next we go. It gets easier all the time.

Then I see Jeanne-Laure sitting in front of a stall where they sell cakes and hot cocoa, thick pea soup and sausages.

The boy lets me go and I glide by myself to the bench on the ice. He is gone, and I haven't even had time to thank this Good Samaritan. On the way back, in the tram, I glow and tingle and feel very happy. 'Isn't it lovely to skate?' I beam at Jeanne-Laure.

1940s
The Country Experience
~
Joyce Harrison

Mr Thomas swung back his wide farm gate and in drove the family of townies for their holiday, their 'country experience'. Stokes Valley seemed quite a distance from Island Bay in a baby Austin, with Grandad's tent poles on the roof and Janne squashed up in the back seat against Grandma's new wooden safe with the gauze door. Then there was all the food and gear for a week's pioneering. They bumped across the bright green paddock bordered by macrocarpas that was to belong to them for a whole week. There was even a cow grazing over by the fence.

Grandad selected a spot to pitch the tent in the shelter of an old barn. Grandma and Janne held up reluctant poles while Grandad drove dozens of wooden pegs into the hard clay. Janne gaped around during this slow process. How still it all was. Huge dark trees like statues; the cow with its head down could be a painting; the grass stiff and bristly. It was not at all like the beach at home with its restless waves and gulls tilting in the wind. Here the air was motionless, buzzing with cicadas that never paused . . .

At last all was shipshape, the sleeping bags bouncy on the slashed tea-tree branches, and a new-style meal clearly if distantly on the way. Given half an hour Janne set off to visit the cow — apparently the only other resident of Stokes Valley, apart from the kind Mr Thomas who was letting perfect strangers camp on his land.

Suddenly, much more exciting than the painted cow, a small, very lively calf bobbed from behind her rump. It stomped over to Janne, clearly wanting to be friends. The cow raised her head for an appraising glance and went back to dragging grass from its tough roots. Janne kept her distance. Did calves bite? Or kick? She ventured a quick pat on the rough head, and then, hearing the call for dinner, assured the calf that she'd be back in the morning.

'Maybe she'll marry a farmer,' Grandad was saying. 'Heaven forbid,' said Grandma, spying out a shady corner for her safe.

The night grew strangely beautiful with a sky full of brilliant stars caged by the branching trees. Later—just their luck—it rained, and they woke to a grey morning. Grandad's tent flap clung wetly to Janne's arm; but when Mr Thomas arrived with a billy of creamy milk their new home seemed cosy as a palace.

The resident animals had retreated further but the calf came lolloping over as soon as Janne appeared. It butted her shoulder and tossed up its gingery head to be patted. Eagerly it began sucking her proffered finger. Janne was indeed startled at the grip of those gummy jaws, and what seemed to be a powerful one-way backward drag. Nervously she imagined her hand and then her arm disappearing into that greedy throat. She pulled away, but now the calf insisted on something more to suck. The mother took no notice of her baby. What could Janne offer? Perhaps the belt of her school raincoat. She unbuckled this and cautiously volunteered a few inches of the harsh fabric.

Jiggling its tail with delight the calf grabbed just as happily at its new tidbit. In fact Janne couldn't quite manage to hang on. The calf appeared to have swallowed the end and to be determined for more. Desperately she hung on, taking a firm grip on the buckle with her other hand. She begged and bullied and even kicked at the calf, but after a final toss of that bony head the end, buckle and all, was whisked from her hands. With one decisive gulp it disappeared down the creature's throat.

Janne was horrified, waiting for the calf to choke or even drop dead on the spot. It had become even more frisky. Could a calf be made to sick up its dinner? Was there perhaps a place in its stomach where the vet could make a little buckle-sized slit? If nothing could be done to get the belt back, was there anything to be gained by confessing, and spoiling her grandparents' carefully planned holiday? On the other hand it would be still worse if Mr. Thomas were to cut open his calf to investigate its sudden death and recognise the belt of her school raincoat! Finally Janne decided to wait and see. She unbuttoned the raincoat to make the absence of the belt less obvious.

Next morning she squirmed when kind Mr Thomas arrived with not only the day's milk but a dear little jar of cream as well. She looked out cautiously. The cow was still grazing. The calf was staring blankly but healthily at the tent.

'Maybe she'll finish up a vet,' Grandad was saying. 'All those questions last night about cows' insides and digestive processes, not to mention the exit hole. I'll have to be doing some homework myself.'

'Hmm,' said Grandma, sniffing her cold corned beef.

The weather had cleared and they set about exploring the hot dry scrub on the hillside, catching katydids and studying stick insects on the tea-tree twigs, and admiring dragonflies shimmering in the sun. At night possums from the barn slid down the tent roof, chattering like seven devils. There were even times when her anxiety was forgotten . . .

'Have you lost interest in the little calf?' asked Grandma.

'I guess it's a naturalist she'll be after all,' said Grandad.

Janne let her surveillance of the calf appear even more casual.

At last the week of buzzing cicadas and marvellous milk came to an end. The gear, now much reduced, was stowed back into the little car. As they jolted back out the gate Janne joined her grandparents in thanking Mr Thomas for his hospitality, and cast a final agonised glance in the direction of the still upright calf.

'What do you think you'll remember most about your country holiday?' asked Grandad.

Janne thought quickly.

'Cream on my Weetbix,' she clowned, and they all laughed.

The holiday had been voted a success.

1930s
The Duck Pond

~

Heather Williams

It's a summer night circa 1931, a summer night that is so hot, it's hard to go to sleep. It's still daylight, and too soon for the sun to go to bed, but my sister and I have been bathed and tucked up in our bed. Why wouldn't we decide that there were better things to do than go to sleep?

Out of bed we crept, through the open window, out the gate, down the hill and guess what!—we were on an adventure, maybe like Peter Pan and Wendy.

The ducks were all hurrying home to their pond, skidding and sliding to a halt as their webbed feet touched down on the surface, applying brakes and announcing their homecoming with loud quacking and flapping of wings. This had to be investigated. More quacking and flapping of wings seemed to invite us to join in the revelry. Why disappoint, after such a cordial invitation?

Off with our nighties and into the lovely cool muddy water we ran.

What fun we had, splashing about, the mud so cool and squelchy between our toes. We made little patterns on the edge of the pond just like the ducks. We made wonderful mud pies and threw handfuls at each other, giggling and laughing, making as much if not more noise than the ducks.

The little yellow ducklings, soft balls of fluff, tickled our hands and feet and tummies. Mother duck didn't seem too pleased about us holding her babies and protested with a great commotion. She flew at us, hoping to make us drop her precious ducklings.

Our mother came to investigate all the noise and found two very grubby little girls who needed bathing all over again.

Like all good things it had to come to an end, but the memories of one summer evening's fun so long ago remain forever.

1940s
Crying
~

Oho Kaa

I woke with a start. Did I hear distant crying or was I dreaming? Bleary eyed, I blinked at the bedside clock. Goodness, it's only 5 o'clock in the morning!

Not fully awake, I grow tense. What on earth is it? Who is that wailing out there? Wide eyed, I sit up and lean forward in my bed. It sounds very much like . . . yes, I do believe it's my mum. There are other voices too.

Clad in my warm pyjamas, careful not to wake my sister, I crawl out of bed to the glass doors. There at the far end of our large verandah is Mum. The cool air and crashing waves of the sea greet me as I make my way to the huddled group. The keening is clearer now. I see three dim shapes, one of them is holding my sobbing mother. As my eyes adjust to the faint light, I recognise my Uncle Sam and Aunty Kura too.

I make my way to my mother and tug at her skirt. 'Don't cry Mum, please don't cry.'

I wrap my arms around her legs hoping maybe it will comfort her and make her stop. She loosens her hold on my uncle and looks down at me. 'It's your Dad, he has been killed. He is in heaven now. Your uncle and aunty have come to break the news to us.'

For a moment my mind is blank, then I glare defiantly at my uncle and aunty. 'You are so mean bringing us news like that! Go away, go away,' I shout. 'I don't like you anymore.'

I slump down on my knees and burst into tears. I feel gentle arms around me pressing me close. They are warm and comforting, but still I weep.

One by one my brothers and sisters venture out and fill the air with broken sobs.

'Why did it have to be you, Uncle, to bring this news to us?' I ask through my tears.

Mum answers for him. 'The postmaster got the call. He knew we would be upset so he thought it would be better if your uncle came instead. So your uncle picked Aunty Kura up and here they are.'

'Why did he get killed?' asks my brother.

Uncle Sam strokes his thin hair, sighing, 'Your dad and his men were in a German trench in Libya. The Germans knew where the trenches were. Their shells were whizzing all around. The men needed food, but were afraid to leave the safety of the trench. So it was up to your dad and a volunteer, Private John Manuel, to get food. They were both shelled. That's war for you.'

'Oh look, the sun is coming up,' pipes my five-year-old sister.

With a heavy heart and tear-filled eyes I follow her gaze. In my imagination, I see my dad walking into the horizon through the glorious sunrise shimmering across the ocean blue.

1930s
The Crossing
~
Shirley Dobbs Signal

I'm a big girl now, all of four years old, and I mustn't cry. Big girls don't make a fuss when they're frightened. But right now my world is a bit shaky. My grandmother, sitting beside me in the back seat of the little car, is also frightened. And somehow I know that in their seats in front of us my mother and father are also afraid. The smell of the dripping bush is heavy and dank, and the rain is pouring down around us. The car's wheels slip and slide on the narrow shingle and mud road. To one side is a steep high bank, on the other a sheer drop to the raging river below. What will stop us plunging over the edge?

Every so often—far too often, it seems—we meet a car coming the other way. One of us has to back up until we find a place wide enough to pass. The engine labours as it struggles to meet the steep and challenging incline. My father is a nervous man, and his fear is so tangible that I feel as if there is another person in the car with us. The smell of the bush, my fear and his terror become tangled together as that other entity.

We left Westport hours ago, heading for Christchurch where a new job is waiting for my father. In 1932 Depression conditions the stark reality is that if he isn't there to start his new job tomorrow morning, he won't have a new job. He won't have a job at all. We have to get over those mountains.

An almost unbearable tension builds inside the car. Mother screams at my father as we slither round a bend in the road . . . I can't take any more. I shut off.

I don't take in anything else until I see that we are in a wide place, with flat ground stretching out to one side of the road. There are mountains all around us, frowning down and through the curtains of driving rain. On the other side of the car stretches a huge river bed, now filled from edge to wide-flung edge with racing, tumbling, roaring brown water. This is the Waimakariri, and it must be a mile wide. Terror builds again . . . we have to cross this river. There is no bridge, won't be one for years, and the usual ford is out. No one can cross these floodwaters.

Father is out of the car, negotiating with a man outside a small tumbledown building. He is very upset, and his arms wave about wildly. The man looks grim, and his arms wave about a bit too. We all have to climb out of the car, and my parents unpack the cases from the boot and pile them on to the back seat. My grandmother and I climb back in and teeter up on to the top of the pile. What now?

As I look around anxiously I see two huge draught horses pulling a big sturdy cart behind them. The grim man, looking even grimmer, is driving them. He reins to a stop, Father carefully drives the car in behind the cart, and together they tie thick ropes from the cart to the car. My mother and grandmother watch this with very white faces. With Father back in the car, the grim man urges his horses towards the river. They balk, they don't want to go into that maelstrom. He yells, flourishes a whip and they reluctantly step forward into that terrifying billow. Too much! — I shut off again!

I become aware that we are out in the middle of what seems to be an endless expanse of floodwater, brown and furious, swinging us

Shirley at Westport on her fourth birthday, with her grandmother.

uncontrollably backwards and forwards behind the cart like a huge and vicious cat tormenting a helpless mouse. The incredible horses pull us on, unfaltering, the grim man clinging to the reins with one hand, to the cart with his other. Water pours inside and across the floor of the car beneath our feet.

We are out there forever; the far side must be nearer than it was! Inch by inch the gap closes until the car is no longer swinging in arcs at the end of the towrope. The wheels have made contact with the gravel underneath and at last the faithful horses drag us up out of the water and on to the side of the road, the Christchurch side.

My father does things to the engine. Water seems to be pouring out of every part of the car. We three females get out, clinging to each other. I don't even notice that the grim man has disappeared—gratitude is not uppermost in my mind.

Much, much later I swim up out of a sound sleep. The thick darkness of a city gone to bed envelops us. Up on the second storey of a large building lights shine out from two large windows. It's Christchurch Hospital. Father glances up and gloomily mutters, 'Some poor sucker getting his stomach cut open.' It's my final dose of fear for the day.

1940s
That Dreaded Walking Stick
~
Oho Kaa

They were huddled round the kitchen table. The only source of brightness came from the hurricane lamp that hung from a Number 8 wire hook attached to the ceiling. The rest of the huge kitchen/dining room was in semi-darkness. The elders were gathered at our home.

It seemed that whenever a group like this met at our home it was for a very special reason. It was like this when my grandmother passed away in February, 1941. Many people had come to stay a few days to comfort us in our grief. I was nearly seven at the time. Now, only a month later, they were here again. Those same people had gathered.

An elder was talking. I listened intently, curious to know why they had come. As I listened it became obvious that someone had had a dream about our house and a tohunga had been called in to interpret the dream. The tohunga lay back with her eyes closed while the dream was being told. I looked around the group. Some bowed their heads, one looked upwards, another was staring straight ahead with her mouth slightly open, another rested her cheek in the cup of her hand. Their thick, dark clothing made them look mysterious and rather scary. Then the voice stopped and there was complete silence. A long silence.

Finally the tohunga made an announcement: there was something in the house that should not be there. A curse had been put on it. If we did not find it, then one by one our whole family would die. I looked around the room. It seemed to have become much darker now. My mother got up, took the hurricane lamp down and gingerly pumped more air into it. It hissed, sending out light that cast huge dancing shadows around the walls as it was returned to its wire hook. There was a buzz of talk for a while. Then the tohunga announced that we had to find whatever it was that very night.

Mum took the lamp again, holding it high. She led the way, with the tohunga close behind her, and we followed her shuffling feet. At each new room, the tohunga would begin chanting. Then she would ask questions, then shake her head and move on to the next room.

We made our way down the long passageway. I was really scared, and stayed close to the group all the way to the front bedroom. The chanting continued throughout. This was the only room left. My mother searched high and low for something strange. She opened the wardrobe, felt into the very corners around its base. There was nothing. She looked along the clothes on hangers, then pushed them all across the bar to one end. She peered intently, and there in the darkest corner was a walking stick. It was carved and painted red. It certainly did not belong to our grandfather.

My mother handed the stick to the tohunga who immediately began earnest incantations over it. Then she looked at us and nodded her head. This was what the dream was about — this was what had been deliberately left behind — a walking stick. She took that walking stick with her and blessed the house before she departed.

Somehow that experience sent chills up my spine, and for a very long time whenever I saw a walking stick I went cold all over. When I went to a marae and saw a walking stick, especially if it was being swung by orators as they marched back and forth across the threshold, I would cower down in fear that they would point the thing at me. I honestly thought I would be struck down.

When I was much older my grandfather would often ask me to get his walking stick for him. I remember the first time I did. I went into his room trembling, looked at the stick, touched it and waited, then held on to it and waited. What a relief to find I was still alive! I saw, too, how the walking stick helped my ageing grandfather. After that it became a real joy to find it for him. I no longer feared it.

1940s
Going to Port Parham
~
Mavis Boyd

All through my childhood we had an annual outing known as the Port Parham trip.

Preparations would begin well in advance with careful consultation of tide tables and long-range weather forecasts and, when all the signs were auspicious, friends and relatives would be invited to join us after morning milking on the appointed day, to travel in convoy on the two-hour journey to the beach.

We lived in the verdant Barossa Valley of South Australia. Port Parham was some fifty miles due west, and there was a gradual but inexorable change of scene as we approached the coastline. In contrast to the gently undulating vine-clad slopes we were used to, we would find ourselves in a flat barren landscape, very hot. The only vegetation: stunted mangroves clustered along a tidal creek, their roots alternately exposed and covered as the tides ebbed and flowed.

This was an inhospitable, uninhabited place, so there had to be a reason for going there. It could be summed up in one word: crabs!

If you followed the outgoing tide (and the shallow water extended for miles) you came across curious blue-black areas like small bruises on the sea bed. When these were disturbed, the chances were that a large blue and white sea crab would come scuttling out, and that was your chance to catch it.

Dad had made for each of us a wooden stick like a broom handle with a claw of spring steel prongs attached to one end. The technique was to prod the smudgy area with the handle and then quickly invert the tool to scoop up the emerging, flailing crab and drop it neatly into the washtub that was tied to Dad's waist by a rope and floated on the water behind him.

The crabs were large and beautiful. Their legs were white underneath and a lovely glistening blue on top. In the water they were very nimble with a peculiar sideways movement. Once in the tub, they were restless, ungainly.

The thrill of the hunt was all-absorbing and by the time we came in for lunch the tub would be well laden. The adults would fill kerosene tins with sea water, kindle a fire and boil the crabs as the centre piece of our meal.

I usually contrived to absent myself from the cooking ceremony. I could hunt and catch crabs with enthusiasm. I could eat them with enjoyment. But I found the idea of their being cooked unbearable. I would busy myself by helping with the other lunch preparations.

Once the crabs were cooked and I was able to feel comfortable in their presence, I marvelled at their size and the way in which all the blue areas had turned orange and red. We would content ourselves with the delicious claws; the rest of the meat would be carefully put aside for later consumption.

We waded out into the sea in old sandshoes in case a crab came out of its hole and nipped our toes. Coming back to the beach I would toss them off—I loved being barefoot, knowing full well how hot the ground would be. I would have to move like lightning, darting from one little patch of shade to the next. I can still recall exactly the feel of the hot baked earth burning my toes as I hopped between the picnic spot, shaded by tarpaulins, and the creek.

Meanwhile the adults might be taking a brief siesta as the children waited impatiently for the tide to come in so that we could swim in the creek. The water was deliciously cool and green with reflected, dancing light. Having Dad swim with us was a special delight. Even then I was aware that such moments of relaxation were rare for him as his days, unlike ours, were filled with labour.

All too soon it would be time to pack up—we had to get home for evening milking. There was always sunburn to be attended to, little ones to be put to bed, another meal featuring crabs, and our Port Parham trip was over for another year.

1940s
A Special Place

~

Kay Carter

We grew up together as brothers and sisters, my cousins, my brother and me. The four of us were real country kids on a farm established in 1865 by the sons of our widowed great-great-grandmother. A country childhood was ordinary for us. We took it for granted and never appreciated how lucky we were, learning so much and having so many adventures.

We were allowed a section of gully for our very own to clear and plant in pine trees. Our fathers had resisted our requests for some time but finally gave in. Our ages would have ranged from nine to twelve, and looking back I am horrified that we were allowed the use of slashers and axes to clear the scrub. It was a short steep climb down the bank to a large flat terrace. We slashed the bracken, gorse and blackberry, breaking up the roots, and leaving the branches to rot.

The creek at the bottom of this gully had a dark rusty flow of water weaving through the scrub and rocks. Nearby was the hydraulic ram with its loud steady thump as it faithfully pumped spring water for the cattle drinking troughs and nearby farm houses. In the larger stream there were freshwater crayfish and eels to be caught and cooked. Not that my mother appreciated, as I did, watching the pieces of eel wriggling in the pan on the stove.

The gully was our own special place. We cleared an area under the big kahikatea tree and built a hut using an old discarded horse cover from our maiden aunt's beautiful big red hunter, Chess. Some of the fertiliser sacks from the implement shed added to our general comfort.

We got up to all sorts of mischief. Peter and Heather would sometimes smuggle in a little of their father's tobacco and we would roll it in thin Zig Zag cigarette papers. We felt terribly ill but grown-up as we tried to smoke them. Still, they were better than dried dock leaves. My brother and I contributed the occasional copy of the newspaper *Truth*, retrieved from where our father had hidden it under the cushions on the settee in the sun porch.

Kay and her dog on the farm.

We would have company on our adventures—our fox terrier and our cousins' Scotch terrier loved to scurry around under the bracken along the banks looking for and disturbing rabbits.

In the spring and summer the field at the top of the bank was often planted with vegetables for the three houses on the farm. This was not a regular vegetable garden, but a strip planted along one side of a field planted with chou moellier for the cows' winter feed. There were rows of peas, turnips, carrots and corn.

Many a long warm evening would be spent picking peas—eating as many as we could manage—and then it was all aboard the trailer, buckets full, to be towed behind the tractor over the fields and home. The produce was then podded and preserved. And not just peas. I can still recall the taste of the cold bottled carrot salad kept in Agee jars in the fridge.

This was the legitimate use of the produce. But many a snack was plucked for a picnic as we hid down the bank under our tree.

Not far from our special place there was a bank of pale blue clay. We had great unrealised visions of this being very special clay that could and should be used to make the finest of china for cups and saucers and plates that we would use on our tables.

One by one, as we grew older, we went away to boarding school. We outgrew our special piece of cleared bank. The small seedling pines we had planted grew, as we did, tall and strong.

1920s
New Year's Eve
~
Jeannette Hunter

The sun is shining. It's warm in the quiet garden where I am playing. What are those noises coming from beyond the fence? I climb on to the roof of the bower in the corner of our garden so that I can look into the courtyard of the college behind our house. The big girls are playing a ball game—should I slide down and join them?

Just then there is another noise: 'Net, Nettie.'

This is annoying. The game is becoming exciting. Any moment now they will throw the ball to me, perched high above them.

'Wake up, Nettie, or you'll be late.'

'No, no, I don't want to wake up, let me sleep, please.'

'Don't you remember, you wanted me to wake you up? It's a quarter to twelve already.'

I stumble out of bed. I know now. It is New Year's Eve. Chel and I have gone to bed early so we can wake up to see in 1928 with the family. I am shivering. It is very cold. Mother gives me a warm dress to put on over my pyjamas, and thick woollen socks. Chel is already dressed, so we go down the two flights of stairs to the dining room together.

The table looks lovely, with a brilliant white tablecloth, a low vase of flowers in the middle, sparkling silver candlesticks and cutlery and by every plate a glass for the red wine my father is just starting to pour. The glasses for Chel and me are three-quarters filled with water, and Father, tipping these glasses slightly, pours in some red wine. From above, it really looks like a glass of wine. On the table are dishes of Russian salad, potato salad, a large flat dish for cold meats, anchovies, gherkins and bowls with nuts and raisins, dates and figs. There are crackers and cheese and my favourite . . . little cubes of very old cheese between several layers of pumpernickel. These are called 'woodcock', for what reason I'm not sure.

'May I have a woodcock, Mum?'

'Not yet, we have to wait for the sign that tells us that it's 12 o'clock.'

Then all the taxis in the city, and the ships in the harbour, start to blow their hooters long and loud. It is a fantastic din of short and drawn-out blasts, high and low, with some explosions of firecrackers to liven it up even more.

'Happy New Year!'

A sip of our wine, hugs and kisses all round, and then we go in a long line upstairs, glass in hand, to wish our grandmother a good year. Chel goes in front, and our father comes last with two glasses of wine so that we can all clink glasses with Oma and drink her health. The telephone rings. My three aunts, sisters of Father and daughters of Oma, are ringing to wish us each in turn, 'A Happy New Year'. This takes a long time and we are getting hungry and impatient.

Downstairs at last we start the year with a cup of hot chicken broth followed by all that delicious food. It is as if my mother, in preparing this feast, has wanted to say, 'I hope that the whole year will continue as we started it.'

After Chel has finished her glass of wine we swap glasses quickly, when nobody is looking, because I don't like wine . . . yet. We can't possibly eat any more so we tumble happy and satisfied into bed, thinking about tomorrow—or is it today?—when we will make a family visit to my mother's parents to wish them, as we do every year, 'A Happy New Year'.

1950s
MTLH
~
Lesley Ferguson

Mother never liked it at Hoi Hoi. 'It's smelly around the bush, it's dark, dank, and dirty, and smells of kerosene,' she'd say. But summer after summer we went there, until the year she finally rebelled.

The old fishing cottage on the bank of the Tauranga Taupo River was fine for devoted fishermen, who patrolled the river and its mouth from four in the morning till eleven at night. Mother suspected that the men stopped by the manuka bush rather than in the outhouse in their haste to maximise fishing time. It was very basic.

A blanket roped off and darkened our corner beds, and we would be there listening while the fishermen yarned at night. 'Why Hoi Hoi?' we wondered, and Father conjectured that as the fishermen (and women) returned in the dark from the river haunts, they'd call to warn of their arrival, 'Hoi Hoi.'

The old unlined bach had been jointly owned for years by Mother's father, her brother Brian, and a couple of other families. When it was being used by one of the others, Mother couldn't be happier. It was a perfect opportunity for us to explore camping spots in the area. And so we found the Tongariro River, and Kowhai Flat, which was our Eldorado. A fabulous swimming hole in a loop of the river, it boasted an island, rapids, and plentiful fishing, not to mention a derelict hut, wild horses, rabbits, white pines, grassy flats . . . and all this for us alone. 'The Queen Mother came fishing here . . . with her double string of pearls,' Mother would remind us, putting her hand to her neck. 'She was Duchess of York, then . . . '

For three successive summer holidays at Kowhai Flat we were the lords of the land. But the fame of Duchess Pool and its wonderful fishing would always, eventually, bring campers, and social conviviality.

Dad would enjoy these animated camping friends, but Mother found such company unnecessary on a holiday. As for my brother and me, we were keen to explore new places, and the lakeside looked exciting.

A week of rainy weather ended our love affair with Kowhai Flat. Floodwater demolished our crescent-shaped swimming pool, the river rose and rumbled its rocks threateningly beside our old tent. We lay on our backs reading, mostly, until Mother came up with the idea of making fudge one day. 'I won't have to get off the bed because everything is at hand,' she pointed out. This was just as well, because any movement in the cramped tent was tricky—no one was allowed to touch the canvas walls, which were scarcely waterproof.

The Primus roared and the ingredients were added as carefully as they could be, when lying flat on one's back. Mum went back to her book while slowly stirring the dissolving sugar. The Primus was slow, but at last the pan reached the boiling stage and, what with the rain and the bubbling, we started to giggle. She had to sit up for the beating process. By the time the fudge was hardened in the enamel plates, we were well into sampling it.

'Very more-ish,' declared Mother, collapsing comfortably on her back. 'Look, I've got some new buttons.' Up her shirtfront lay a row of fudge buttons—a very convenient reading snack. We giggled till we cried. I don't think the men got the joke—or much fudge.

Our next camp lacked the great trees and grassy flat, but overlooked the whole lake, and we felt like real pioneers. We burrowed into the manuka trees and scrub to clear a small area near the lake, and set up two tents and our manuka pole kitchen. This boasted a shaky bench, racks for towels and pots, a toilet washing area and various other refinements, improvised fresh each day. We would hang butter, cheese, meat, lettuce and milk in dampened flour bags nearby, hooked under the trees. Privacy was precious, so every time we drove in or out of camp in Mission Bay, John and I replaced manuka scrub branches over our entrance. These of course withered noticeably after a few days.

There were glassy sunny days in the bay, and sometimes surf-pounding days, days that brought restless, wave-thumping nights. But best of all were the velvet starry nights. Never had stars been so awesomely plentiful, so bright, so enticing. Twilight walks were a must. We would stroll up the road above the lake, lingering to admire the sparkling spread of water, and then swivelling our heads around to gaze up at the Milky Way. It was on one such evening stroll that we noticed the FOR SALE sign.

An old bach stood at the rear of the rankly grassed section. There

McKenzie family and friends in early days at Hoi Hoi.

were some grapevines, and a graceful red gum tree near the front. We took to walking that way often.

At Easter that year, we went back to our camping spot by the lake and our aunt Monica came with us. Now we had three great cooks in camp, including a dietician. Some of the things we had to eat, though, were somewhat impaired by the hot weather. Father said the troops would have thought them delicacies, in his army days. Skipping our plates out into the lake after meals to wash them was a neat trick. Such freedom was only possible at remote places such as this.

Our walks now nearly always took us past the funny old bach. It had brown weatherboards and windows all along its face. And there was an unusual sloping ramp, like a collapsed deck, at the front. What was it for? Was it all a garage? The whole face seemed to be removable, so perhaps the owners drove up the ramp? These questions were never answered. But, as the months went by, an idea grew. By Christmas that year, 1956, Monica had contacted the solicitors in Wanganui about removing the FOR SALE sign. The first thing Father wanted to know was whether it was for sale freehold. This was the first time I learned about leasing, or Māori ownership of land.

By 1957 the bach was ours, and our excitement cannot be described. Father took out a second mortgage to buy it, and we all paid in what we could from our salaries. Mother was working at Turners & Growers, I was at the Ministry of Works nursery, my brother was survey contracting around Taihape, and Monica was a nutritionist with the Health Department. Every Friday, or Saturday morning, she would come in with the Taupo account notebook, and we would pay our contributions. We were shareholders in a great enterprise!

Gradually, over the years, the mortgage was paid off. We looked on the bach as giving us a more luxurious style of camping. We were certainly not short of carpet. The previous owners, the Tricketts, had been carpet importers, and had stitched together numerous carpet samples to create multicoloured floor mats. There was also an enormous and unique durrie rug that became a much loved item in the cottage. Mother christened the place MTLH (Mr Trickett's Little House), and so it remained till she died.

MTLH boasted an earth closet, gas lights, a water tank outside, a cupboard full of Greydawn Johnson blue china (the most complete set of china I had ever seen), a string-and-nail door latch (which all children loved to play with), and the most enormous fireplace, with a rod and hooks to hang the billy on. The pit toilet was approached along a narrow pumicy path by the rear lawson hedge, which dripped on you as you brushed past. Best, and worst, was the hole itself. Below the seat grew a lovely fringe of ferns, but before the ferns started, the pumice walls were home to wetas—bush wetas with very long feelers which could be seen waving in the torch-light. Some children refused to use the toilet, but in fact it was bearable once the smell of Jeyes Fluid had taken over, and Dad had bombed the mosquitoes. I never went there without taking a torch, and a brush and shovel to attack spiders.

Why Mum had been so fussy about the Hoi Hoi lav, I'll never know. She once dropped her precious glasses down the terrible hole at MTLH and in desperation quietly went out with her fishing line and torch to try to retrieve them. Plenty of giggles and tears over that!

There was no plumbing, so washing was done in a basin on a bench we built outside. Water left in the bowl overnight had frequently turned to thick ice on winter mornings—complete with drowned and frozen heu heu moths. Even when the men made improvements to the plumbing and cooking facilities, it was still 'luxury camping', as Mother described it. But those holidays were the happiest of family times.

1930s
Snails
~
Joyce Harrison

Our maiden aunt was great value. Her four nieces and nephews reckoned that if she had had *ten* children of her own she couldn't have been better at the things for which we appreciated her: remembering the names of our friends and keeping track of our hobbies and inventions, not to mention being always ready to applaud our successes. I particularly enjoyed her zany side, and her willingness to forget about time while we studied such fiddly things as cicada cases, and the fluttery petticoats beneath ladybird wings.

She and my grandpa lived in the family home along with Emily, who had been the family help for many years. Emily would raise a despairing eyebrow to guests when meals were delayed at Aunt's behest, or when confiding her difficulty in getting her vacuum into Aunt's 'horror room'. (This was a cavern forbidden even to me, containing Aunt's piles of newspaper clippings, drafts of her articles, and her collection of miscellaneous treasures, which was reported to be steadily growing.)

The house had been designed long ago by one of my uncles. It had an elaborate wooden latticework surround on the verandah, and in the sitting room a huge fireplace. I can dimly remember my old grandpa huddled over the fire with his pet saucepan, from which he spooned up his own concoction of soup known to the family as 'ashmigoo'. He played alternately his two favourite records: 'Laughing Gas' with Cecily Courtnedge, and Stanley Holloway's 'Albert and the Lion'. On the sideboard a bell jar housed a faded orange-eyed bird. Alongside stood the huge and precious radiogram with its own glowing eye.

Auntie would lean back in her cane armchair on the porch, waving her arm over the massed and mixed flowerbeds which overflowed onto paths and up fruit trees. She called it her cottage garden. My mother used to murmur that she would call it something else, which I could never quite catch. To me, as a small child, it was an idyllic playground.

Holidays with Auntie were worth the bumpy night on the Limited that ended with the grey rush of the Auckland platform, and a friendly face peering in at the window. She would have been keeping in touch since the previous visit by means of colourful letters, carefully printed and edged with a cavalcade of animals and flowers cut from old postcards and magazines.

What I liked best of all at her place was pottering with her in that Greenlane garden. Although only a stone's throw from the Great South Road, which even in the 1930s was a busy highway, her place was alive with birds and creepy-crawlies. My favourites were the snails, whose relatives had not yet crawled their way to Wellington, or at least not to our part of town.

On one visit, when I was about seven, the snails were everywhere. 'Naked ladies', we called them, admiring the way their clothes were rolled up on their backs, as they returned along the concrete from their dip in the morning dew—a private joke, this, among many jokes which would no doubt have been regarded as unseemly for publication in the Children's Page of the *New Zealand Herald*, of which Auntie was the popular editor. It was after this visit, however, that she overstepped the mark—even for me.

A few days after our return home, a parcel arrived with Auntie's handwriting spread boldly across the top. Had we left something behind? The package had come airmail so must be urgent. Yet it was light as a feather. Laboriously we untied the knots and unwrapped the brown paper of those pre-plastic days. Inside was a waxed cardboard honey pot with a note on top:

> Thursday
>
> Dear Sunshine,
> Didn't we have fun! I thought you might like these for pets and as a reminder of your holiday.
> Lots of love,
> Auntie
>
> P.S. There are plenty more.

A clown in the bottom corner waved at me with innocent glee.

There were holes punched in the side of the pot. I backed off. Mum cautiously prized off the frayed cardboard lid and we looked in. From among the wilted sprigs of greenery there arose first one and then half a dozen pairs of swaying stalk eyes. Soon the inside wall of the pot was alive with snails squirming their way to the light, balancing in twos and threes along the round lip and negotiating the steep descent. We watched aghast as they dispersed themselves like living blobs of phlegm across the white oilcloth of our kitchen table. How would Dad react to one more pest to add to our woodlice and white butterflies? Mum quietly but promptly disposed of the newcomers, but I could not so easily quell my squamous dreams.

> Sunday.
>
> Dear Auntie,
> Thank you very much for sending the snales. They were a big surprise. The snales were very well thank you and came out strate away.
> Love from
> Sunshine.
>
> P.S. That was plenty thank you.

1930s
The Ball
~
Jeannette Hunter

The whole class was abuzz. All those fourteen-year-olds could speak of nothing else: there was going to be a school ball. To say 'the whole class' is a bit misleading, I suppose, for the seven boys in the class of twenty girls would probably have been far more interested had they been invited to a soccer match!

June, like most of her classmates, had gone to dancing lessons during the winter months. She started off protesting that dancing wasn't anything for her. How little she knew herself. She really loved it, and knew she was good at it, because the dancing master often asked her to help him demonstrate a new step. They learned the foxtrot, the quick-step, the tango, rhumba and English waltz, and the Viennese waltz too. These waltzes, slow and quick, were her favourites. It was all very elegant and fluent, nothing like the angular, staccato, twisty movements of later years.

What dress to wear? June and her mother devoured all the fashion magazines and catalogues—*Vogue* and *McCall's*. So many beautiful ball gowns, what to choose? In the end it was not so difficult, because the one she was going to have jumped out of the page at her: little white fleecy summer clouds in a bright blue sky!

They bought very fine open white lacy material with white leaves on long slim stems, and a lovely cornflower blue taffeta to go underneath it. The dressmaker assured them that she would have the gown ready in time.

At school the girls knew exactly what their friends were going to wear. They showed each other scraps of material and explained or drew how their dresses were going to look, while pretending to be very busy writing or reading.

Carla talked about her raspberry-red velvet gown while she peered—or so she made out—through a microscope.

The biology teacher, coming past, asked her: 'What have you got underneath?'

Carla, reddening, stuttered: 'Only a singlet, Sir.'

The bewildered teacher looked silently at the microscope and then gave a trumpeting laugh. The girls teased Carla for years about this misunderstanding.

At last the night of the ball arrived. Mother helped June to dress. First the blue underdress with the little buttons at the back, then the tight-bodied overgown with the little puffed sleeves and the gathered skirt, a blue taffeta sash around her tiny waist with a large bow at the back, and her mother's blue necklace around her bare neck. The white shoes did not feel as good as they looked but, since her mother had always told her: 'Who wants to be beautiful has to suffer,' she was quite prepared to put up with that tiny inconvenience.

She floated downstairs like a little cloud, the taffeta rustling mysteriously.

'Ta-ra!' She threw open the sitting-room door.

Her father, looking up from his newspaper, said absentmindedly, 'Very nice, June.'

Her eldest sister said, as she had so many times before as 'a joke', '*Sweeeet*, but stupid!'

So much for their support and encouragement.

The hall at school was decorated with streamers and flowers and it looked very festive. There was a small band playing on the stage. All the girls clustered on one side of the hall, admiring each other's dresses. The boys, on the other side, looked much better than they did in the classroom. Then June's heart gave a quick bound: there was Gerard, his curly hair not very tidy, even tonight, but still looking much smarter than all the other boys. He was two years her senior and she didn't think he knew of her existence. Would he dance with her? Would anyone dance with her? When a boy looked at her she looked away and started an animated conversation with the girl next to her.

Then a teacher asked her to dance. What a relief! He had no feeling for rhythm whatsoever, but if she chattered a lot to drown out the music, she could follow his awkward steps without stepping on his toes, or tripping over her own feet. Later, a classmate danced with her and then — miracle of miracles — Gerard took her onto the floor. She was floating, too happy to talk, when she suddenly came down with a crash. The boy she liked least in her class had tapped Gerard on his shoulder. It was an 'excuse me' dance!

After that, June mingled with the flowers on the wall. She did not want to be seen sitting there, so she spent her time going to comb her hair or getting something to eat. The smile on her face fixed itself increasingly into a groove as it got later.

The last dance was a 'leap year' dance, or a 'ladies' choice'. Her last chance to dance her English waltz. Whom could she choose? The boys who had not asked her obviously didn't want to dance with her. The boys who had didn't want to be her partner again, surely? In the end she let her favourite dance slip by . . .

Her father came to pick her up at midnight. 'And how was it, June?'

'Fantastic, really lovely!' she said brightly.

1940s
The Long, Dark Night
~
Oho Kaa

There is a black out. World War II has moved into the Pacific, close to Aotearoa. Our huge house is in complete darkness. I have helped Mum fasten our darkest blankets to all our windows. The news on the radio has warned us — no lights after dark; cover all windows as an extra precaution.

We are quite close to the sea. That alone is enough to scare the daylights out of anyone. My sister and I are huddled in our bed, our three brothers in the next room, Grandad in his own room and our Mum way down at the far end of the house.

I am lying very close to my sister. She is younger than me, yet to know that she is close makes me feel a little braver. But not much. My eyes are tight shut, my mind's eye wondering if any warships are passing by. I pull my knees up closer to my chin. Would those Japanese soldiers come to our house first? There is a house closer to the beach than ours—perhaps they will go there first. I say a prayer, 'Please God, don't let them come and get us.'

If only my Dad was here. But he has been killed, never to come back. Mum is here, but will she be able to fight off those soldiers? Will my Grandad? I pray and pray.

I hear the crashing waves, the rustling trees. Our dog Billy-o barks, I push myself down under the blankets. I pull the sheet over my head. Then all is quiet. I squeeze my eyes tighter, trying hard to sleep. I toss and turn. I hear the waves and sea again. I use my pillow to block out all the sounds of this long dark night. As I wait anxiously for the dawn to arrive I fall into a dreamless sleep.

1940s
The Elephant
~
Shirley Dobbs Signal

An elephant lives under our house. He's been there for years, and given no trouble at all—hibernating perhaps? We would still be unaware of his existence but for the fact that for some reason or other he has become uncomfortable. So he does what we all do. He turns over.

Now an elephant is a creature of some bulk, and if he turns that amount of bulk, his surroundings are going to notice something. We do! We're all woken out of sound sleeps by an incredible bouncing sensation. We scream. The elephant is still not as comfortable as he would like to be. He turns over again. Pandemonium breaks out. Glass shatters, bricks tumble, furniture dances around the rooms—we scream again.

My father is at Wigram Air Force Base in the South Island. My grandmother, my mother and I are above the elephant in Island Bay, Wellington. It's mid-1942. The Japanese, we are sure, are stealthily cruising Cook Strait waiting for a chance to land, sweep up the Parade, and annihilate us all. A submarine has already been reported out there, skulking. On top of all this, who needs elephants—especially restless elephants?

My mother detects some added distress in my grandmother's calls and she runs to her room. My grandmother is having a heart attack. The elephant, meanwhile, just can't seem to find a comfortable position. He stretches his back legs, he stretches his front legs, he moves his head around. I'd swear he's waving his trunk around!

I'm summarily routed out of bed. 'Get dressed, quickly! You'll have to run to Dr Sternberg's house!' Very few people have phones in their homes and the elephant has probably messed up the system. I tremble my way out into the black night and try to run along the road. It is not easy. One of the most difficult obstacle courses I've encountered up to now is the heaving pavement. Fortunately I am unaware of dangling lines or dislocated tramlines. I arrive at the poor doctor's front door, pounding on it and crying in great gasps. Yet he doesn't hesitate — just grabs his little black bag and runs back with me.

(I realise later that he and his family must have been just as terrified as we were — it turns out that they, along with thousands of other people, had an elephant under their home, too.)

My grandmother is pretty sick. She's had a very hard life, and is now seventy-two. She doesn't have many reserves. We get her as comfortable as possible and the doctor promises to come back first thing in the morning. My mother and I have a vague look round the house and simply can't take in the enormity of what has happened. We climb back into her bed, and cower there.

Amazingly, I sleep! When I open my eyes in the morning two red-hot daggers strike into them. I can't stand the light. Eyes tightly shut in case the knives strike again, I try to get out of bed. I can't do that either — my legs refuse to do their normal job! My mother comes over to check on me. Although I can't look at it, her face must be a study. I'm covered in spots. At fourteen years of age, I've chosen this time to go down with English measles!

My father is granted compassionate leave, but he can't get transport for a day or so. Meantime, my poor mother is on her own, nursing two invalids in the midst of utter confusion.

Both chimneys have collapsed, and the rooms are piled high with bricks and soot. The large pantry in the kitchen is walk-in no longer, but filled shoulder-high with a lethal mixture of broken glass, syrup from preserves, the preserves themselves, shattered crockery, honey, golden syrup, milk from the safe, oatmeal, flour — you name it, it's there, all inextricably mixed together. Pictures and ornaments are down from walls and mantelpieces. Broken glass and china threaten unshod feet all through the house.

My case of measles is severe — the nocturnal dash for the doctor probably hasn't done me much good. I'm off in a world of high temperatures and misery, and not taking much in. I am aware of how the trivial can inflame in times of stress. My mother is furious with the

EPS wardens as they clamber over our roof—as well as hundreds of others, no doubt—clearing the remains of the chimneys and hurling the bricks down on to her precious lawn, chewing up the grass no end.

None of us has heard of such things as earthquake survival kits—we are not even earthquake conscious, although heaven knows why not, in our land. After all, it's only eleven years since the Napier quake, and the Murchison one was not too long before that. How my mother copes I can't imagine, but I'm not wondering much as I swim half-conscious through the next two days. Eventually Dad arrives, but I'm not much into even noticing that.

By the time I'm allowed out of bed, the incredible shambles has mostly been cleaned up. Unbelievably there haven't been any fatalities, although the quake measured well over 6.0 on the Richter scale. Had it occurred during the daytime, it would probably have been a different story. There are photographs in the paper—large chunks of concrete parapet down all over the city streets, and broken glass everywhere.

I lie resting in bed thinking that although I'm glad I've lived through the elephant's tantrums, I'm also glad not to be involved in the herculean effort of restoring our household to order. I know I'll never forget the sheer terror of that night, when I had to push aside my fear because there was a job to do and I was the only one who could do it.

And most of all I'll never forget the turning over of the elephant!

1940s
Boys in Khaki

~

Mavis Boyd

I was twelve years of age when war was declared, old enough to realise that we were caught up in a horrifying drama that would affect our lives in ways over which ordinary people had no control. Young men from the district went off to war, but nobody in my immediate family was of an age to be affected.

Life had to go on. I started high school. We were aware that some German folk who had arrived in our district recently had been interned, probably without any justification, and would have to spend the war years in confinement. We were not greatly affected by the food rationing, as we produced a lot of our own. As we always wore hand-medowns, clothes rationing was, for us, a non-event. On one occasion a teacher said to the class, 'I have wool and needles here, and I would like volunteers from among the girls to start knitting scarves, mittens or balaclavas for the soldiers. If you would like to help please see me at the end of the period.' I squirmed uncomfortably in my seat. My knitting was not very accomplished, and the challenge seemed too daunting, so I lay low.

Inevitably there was news of someone in the district having been killed, or missing in action, and I experienced a mixture of sadness and anger that a young life had been cut down. It seemed obscene that these lives had to be sacrificed, in much the same way as that of the beautiful young girl who had to be sacrificed to the monster in the fairy stories.

To raise money for the war effort the community had a series of concerts in the Town Hall, drawing on local musical talent including the A Grade brass band. Other small groups performed skits or short plays, church choirs polished up some items, individuals dusted off their 'cellos or flutes and practised for the next 'get-together'. They were splendid concerts, and the items we enjoyed most were eagerly discussed on the drive home.

In late 1942 there was a dramatic change: the new threat from Japan that made Australia seem very vulnerable. Australians had been serving in the Middle East for some time, but in the light of this development they were brought home to be sent up to Queensland and New Guinea in case of invasion. The authorities thought that they should be given some recreational leave before they went to another battle zone, but instead of sending them to their homes they decided to billet them in the Barossa Valley for a few weeks. Every household in the town was given an allocation according to the number of bedrooms they had. Suddenly the normally quiet town was alive with uniformed figures.

It was enormously exciting for a fourteen-year-old. Living on a farm and cycling five miles to school and home again was all right as far as it went, but now the town was swarming with soldiers, all of whom to my young eyes looked like film stars. At school I spent my time daydreaming. I would be the heroine who, just by chance, bumped into one of these god-like creatures—my mind would weave a Technicolor cinematic fiction around these images, while the Algebra teacher droned on.

Probably inevitably, but to me quite surprisingly, romance blossomed—though not for me. My aunts who lived in town were hosting three soldiers and of course we were anxious to look them over. My eldest sister Doris was eighteen at the time, and the first time we met our aunts' guests it was obvious that Bob, one of the trio, had eyes only for her. When she suggested tentatively that they might like to see our farm, Bob replied, 'When can I come? Tomorrow?'

He came, and all the younger sisters clustered around, listening to stories of his exploits and his experiences in the war.

'Look at the way he can blow smoke rings,' my younger sister said admiringly.

They were heady times. One day I went into town with my father to get the mail, and we stood on the pavement watching two soldiers walking casually along. My attention was attracted as if by a magnet to anything male and in uniform, but Dad was observing something else. As we watched the lithe young figures with their upright carriage, he said quietly, 'Just look at that. You are watching men who know how to march. That's professional training for you.'

Just for that moment, Dad spoke to me as though I was adult and equal. The memory stayed with me long after the incident that sparked it had been all but forgotten.

Then as suddenly as the influx began, it ended. At the end of the third week of their leave, the soldiers were told they were moving on to Queensland.

There was general regret among the hosts and the guests. The townspeople had been happy to show hospitality to the soldiers, the soldiers had enjoyed the contrast from the hot arid Middle East, and the young girls with their heads filled with romantic ideas had delighted in it. Doris and Bob were in love, and a year later, when he got leave, Bob returned and they were married. A city boy and a country girl. He went back to his unit but eventually returned and took up life on an irrigation block growing oranges—theirs was not the only example of a wartime encounter changing the pattern and direction of people's lives.

Before the war ended my cousin George perished, when the HMAS *Perth* was torpedoed by the Japanese. Eventually the soldiers came home, among them some who had been prisoners of war. One such prisoner was welcomed home one night when I was at a dance. He was cheered and someone made a speech. His response was to stare back at us, sombre and unsmiling. His expression sent a little chill through me.

The war did not affect us as much as it did some others, but over those years it was very much there, in the background of our lives. When it ended, with the atomic bomb, it took us some time to realise that the world would never be the same again.

1940s
One Down, Two to Go . . .
~
Heather Williams

As a whisper of breeze stirs the curtain, and a finger of light pokes through the window, I become aware of stirrings in the household. The bleating of sheep in the yard reminds me that today the shearers arrive to begin their work . . . but not without a pre-breakfast cup o' tea to ready them for a 5.30 a.m. start. It's time to tumble out of bed.

Grandpa has already lit the fire in the stove and the kettle is puffing welcoming clouds of steam into the kitchen as I sleepily emerge from my bedroom. Today I am the 'chief cook and bottlewasher' with the task of providing the shearers, and everyone else, with meals and endless cups of tea. The realisation of what is before me banishes any remaining sleepiness.

There is 'woman's work' to be done and I'm the only one to do it. (It's three years since my Nanna died; and Mother is away, as is the housekeeper.) No matter that I am just fifteen years old—I am the right gender, so the question of choice doesn't arise. It's just the way things are. It is 1942, the war is in full swing and two shearers have been employed and need feeding. None of this lessens the trepidation I feel.

Breakfast consists of porridge, sausages, bacon and eggs, tea and toast, all of which has to be ready by 8 a.m. sharp, when Grandpa and my uncles return from milking, and the shearers come in for their first break for the day.

The meal eaten, the shearers return to the shed. Grandpa keeps the fire supplied with barrowloads of wood, one of my uncles and my sister are kept busy for most of the day returning the shorn sheep to the paddock and replacing them with newly mustered ones. A never-ending cycle.

Clearing up after the meal and washing the dishes, the next task is to prepare 10.30 morning tea. I pile wood into the firebox to heat up the range oven ready for a batch of scones to be served buttered and topped with raspberry jam. That out of the way, preparation starts on the midday meal: lamb or mutton, vegetables and a dessert, to be ready and served on the dot.

I'm halfway through the day—so far, so good. But it's now time to whisk up a cake to bake while slices of bread are cut and buttered for sandwiches at 3 o'clock. In spite of having the window and the door wide open, the heat of the kitchen, and the day outside, is beginning to tell. I'm feeling rather tired, but the day's not over yet.

Late in the afternoon the shearers finish up, but my uncles and Grandpa come in for tea and sandwiches before going off to milk the cows.

It's now dark and the men have returned to the house, ready to sit down to another hot meal—lamb or mutton again, with vegetables. The dishes are done, the kitchen cleaned up, and then, thankfully, to bed.

One day gone, two to go . . .

1930s
Moortje
~
Jeannette Hunter

Mother came home full of enthusiasm: she had found the perfect holiday home for us. It was a small cottage, on the edge of a lovely pine forest, with a beautiful view over a golden undulating carpet of wheat. It wasn't far away which was a great advantage as we didn't have a car. In 1931 most people in Amsterdam didn't have cars.

Days before we were due to go, we packed our personal treasures: books we wanted to read, games to play, balls, racquets and so on. The two eldest sisters probably packed their own clothes, but Mother helped us 'littlies' to sort ours out. I remember my little cane suitcase with its loops and toggles as fasteners.

How we got to the place I can't remember, but it must have been quite a move with all our luggage and our cat 'Moortje' in his little cage. We would have left him at home with the neighbours, as we always did in the holidays, but this time he wasn't very well. Moortje was a well-loved member of our family and we could not bear to leave him alone and sick.

By the time we arrived, the legendary waves of golden grain in front of our holiday place had turned into a field of untidy stubble, and when the wind blew we couldn't see even that, because of sand or dust blowing everywhere.

This 'find' of my mother's was a source of hilarity for years to come.

Poor Moortje wasn't getting any better, so one day the vet was asked to come. Just before he arrived, my mother sent me to get the groceries from the village shop. Nobody told me anything, but I had a strange feeling that I knew what was going to happen while I was out. When I came home and found my forebodings to be true I screamed at my parents in fury and grief and collapsed sobbing on my bed. I felt badly betrayed.

My father came later into my room to tell me that Moortje would have become more and more ill and that we did not want him to be in pain. I looked up at him and saw tears in his eyes. The anger disappeared but the sadness stayed for quite some time.

1940s
Camping
~
Lesley Ferguson

Who hasn't got a camping story?

It was the first summer after the war, so we had Father with us again. Adventure and the unknown beckoned. 'Tongapurutu' was the destination, according to Mother.

'You say Tongapuroot, without the U,' said Father. 'It's not far from New Plymouth.'

'Timbuctoo,' muttered John and I. We thought he was teasing us.

We were going in Dad's pride and joy, a Morris 8 sports car that had been released by the Army. It was khaki coloured when he bought it but, scrape by scrape, we all rubbed down the little car until one day it was a deep shiny blue, with chromium trim. It was very small for four people and their camping gear.

In the grey light of dawn on the morning of departure the assembled gear was packed with military efficiency. Mother and John were stowed first into the front left seat, and I was crammed into the space behind them with all the camping gear. Beside me were the Emergency Petrol Can, the ham, the spade and the toilet paper, not to mention the bags and cooking gear. All of this was firmly secured in place under a tarpaulin. Oh, yes, and a last-minute addition for me to clutch was

John's fishing box (nearly forgotten). Painfully crafted from splintery apple-box wood with leather strip hinges, it had a strong fishy smell which reminded me of our holiday at the Sounds last year, when my brother was the 'man of the family' with Father still fighting overseas. The fish and petrol smell were soon blown away, fortunately.

Past rivers, hedges and bridges, beaches, cliffs and paddocks we drove until, cramped and windblown, we stopped to marvel at the concrete canoe and warriors outside the Town Hall of a rural town. Patea.

'Not long, now,' said Dad, and we all sang 'Bless 'Em All' and 'I've Got Sixpence'. We soon knew every verse. Tongapurutu at last? Not much to welcome weary travellers! One shop and . . . ?

A lovely grassy paddock beckoned us. 'Ask the farmer,' we shouted. 'Ask him.' And so we opened the gate and crushed through the long grass. We stopped beside a tall cabbage tree, and made camp.

'Everyone pulls their weight,' said Father, used to military precision. Poles and ropes soon propped up our tarpaulin, the groundsheet went down, and the valise with its red-striped army blanket inside took pride of place. A knapsack and a duffle bag full of clothes completed the furnishings.

Mother's clothes were at the bottom of the duffle bag, Dad's were on the top and Mum called this makeshift camping wardrobe 'the Big Dig'. She wasn't very happy about it.

Then came the kitchen: halved kerosene tins for washing, soap shaker, small primus, enamel plates, and a butter-box for utensils. Our camp looked lonely and little in the grassy expanse under the lone cabbage-tree. A dozen curious cows munched around the lean-to tarpaulin.

'There is nothing like eating in fresh air,' raved our parents while we squatted to eat our ham, potato and salad. 'Al fresco,' said John. There is nothing quite like eating ham which has travelled all day next to a fumy can of emergency petrol.

We walked after tea out onto soaring grey cliffs—which fell dramatically to the black beach below, leaving one's stomach lurching in space. Along the roadside cuttings, high above the sea, were lodged sea creature shapes and shells. 'Fossils,' said John wisely, and the theme took hold. 'Dinosaurs, I expect,' said Mother. 'And now it's back to dinerplates.' We headed back to our paddock. 'Dinersaurs, dinerplates,' chanted John and Mother, chummy and exasperating. They were anxious to tidy up the kitchen before dark. My usual, and the worst, job was to collect the kindling.

Setting off in Dad's ex-Army Morris 8.

'The tarp is down,' shouted John, enjoying the maleness of his newfound army slang. 'Oh dear, the cows must have done it,' said Dad. As we righted the camp chaos it became apparent that the Thermos cork was missing, as was the cork for the thermette. I could hear the nearby cows' stomachs rumbling. 'Corker cows,' said John. 'We will just have to let them work this one out,' said Dad.

It took two more summers, two more hams and two Christmas puddings before they learned that, to keep me happy, the food and the petrol would have to travel in less matey circumstances. And the duffle bag? To keep Mother happy, that too became a thing of the past.

1950s
First Day at St Joseph's

~

Oho Kaa

As the last verse of 'There's a Track Winding Back' drifted through the bus, we drove slowly up the long gravelled drive to St Joseph's Māori

Girls' College. A huge spreading date palm offered us welcome shade from the burning sun. We claimed our bags from the grassy verge and were ushered inside, through a long passageway and into a large room where we were formally welcomed by the nuns and older students.

A few ground rules were laid before us: no running inside, no wearing shoes upstairs, no shouting inside. Then we were each assigned to one of the older students. My cousin Miriama took charge of me. She helped me with my bag and showed me where to put my shoes before we went upstairs in our stockinged feet to the dormitories. A numbered locker had already been allotted to me, so Miriama moved quickly round the thirty-bed dormitory to suss out a good mattress and bed position for me.

'Throw your cardigan on this one. It's in a good place, not too close to the windows and you are not hemmed in by all those beds,' she said with a satisfied sweep of her arms. We then unpacked my bag. Two of everything went into my locker and the third went into the special cupboard out on the landing where one of the nuns ticked off my name. 'This cupboard will only open on Saturdays,' she explained.

Next, my cousin helped me with my bed. Her movements were quick and matter-of-fact as she tucked in the edges so smoothly. 'Now, each Saturday, you strip off the bottom sheet for the wash, put your top sheet on the bottom and whoever is on duty will give you your spare sheet.' My new white counterpane looked neat and tidy on my bed.

Then suddenly an alarm-like bell rang. It rang continuously. 'Better go down now. Put your slippers on—Sister will keep ringing the bell till all the girls are down.' My slippered feet followed the rest of the flock. I was puzzled by this word 'Sister'. Girls seemed to be hurrying from everywhere. I thought to myself, 'It's just as well the stairs are wide.' Everyone moved quickly and quietly. The bell stopped ringing when the girls were lined along both walls of the long passageway. Not a sound was to be heard. Everyone stood. A nun stood at the far end of the passageway. Her voice boomed out, 'Good evening, everyone.'

'Good evening, Sister.' So that's what a sister is, I thought—a nun. My mind was preoccupied with this name, Sister, while a prayer was being said. It was much later that I learnt the true meaning of Sister—like the Sisters of Mercy and Sisters of Compassion.

In the refectory, Sister announced, 'For this meal you may sit wherever you please, but after tomorrow you will sit where directed.' All the tables seated eight girls and had white starched tablecloths, a small vase of flowers on each. Set in each place was a dinner plate with two slices of meat, and a bowl of rice pudding with a blob of whipped cream. A large bowl of potatoes and a large bowl of veges sat in the centre.

When Sister was sure that everyone had a place at table, grace was said in unison. Many girls made the sign of the cross and when the grace finished they did it again. Then we sat down to our first meal. No talking seemed to be the order. Sister walked round while we ate. On finishing our meal we waited for the word to stand. A thanksgiving grace was said, then we all filed out.

We explored the classrooms, the music rooms, bathrooms, sassi room (a little room where we had to wash our homemade sanitary towels) and sewing room, while listening hard to all the tips given by the older students. That night as I lay in my bed another cousin of mine came to see me. I was feeling quite brave and at home when suddenly she said, 'Now don't you cry, will you. I did when I first came here.' And believe it or not I did cry myself to sleep.

1940s
Mother's Curtains
~
Rachelle Calkoen

During the German occupation of Holland we—the Dutch—had to cope with a shortage of food and clothing, soap and paper. There were coupons for almost everything: bread, butter, cigarettes *or* sweets (you couldn't have both), meat, fruit, other edibles and also textiles.

My mother had been fortunate enough to buy some material without having to hand over her precious textile coupons. The light brown flimsy fabric was enough to make curtains for her bedroom, and she started immediately to cut them to the right size and, after hauling the heavy hand-sewing machine out of the cupboard, proceeded to hem them.

She noticed that the material was quite grubby and decided to wash them before hanging them. Domestic washing machines didn't exist and all our washing was sent out. Mother would count the dirty washing, note it down on a specially printed washing list and put it in a large cane basket with a sturdy cane lid held shut with an iron bar that fitted through four leather loops. It was picked up every Monday and returned the following Wednesday, clean and neatly folded. Father's shirts and the tablecloths were starched, ironed and folded with a blue ribbon around them. Everything then had to be counted again and crossed off the washing list. So you will gather that there was not much in the way of washing that went on in our household.

But the curtains. Mother put them in a pot and sat it on the stove to heat up the soapy water. It was not real soap, of course—that didn't exist anymore—but a substitute.

That day I came home late after the whole family had already had lunch. Mother said, 'I kept some soup for you, Rachelle. It's probably still hot.' Hungry—I was always hungry at that time—I looked in the saucepan, turned the heat up, gave the soup a good stir, added a bit of water because it seemed a bit too thick, and filled my plate quite full. It tasted pretty awful but I wasn't amazed about that, because we had to use all substitute ingredients and most food or drinks tasted quite nasty.

Mother came into the kitchen, looked at the nearly empty saucepan and exclaimed, 'What happened to this?'

I said, 'I'm eating it.'

'But child,' she wailed, 'you're eating my curtains!'

1940s
Tanunda Creek

~

Mavis Boyd

Our vineyard nestled at the foot of a range of hills. During the summer these hills would become flaxen as the hot sun bleached the grass, but after the winter rains they were green with lush grass, which smelt of freshness and sap. Each spring we used to climb up into these hills to a favourite picnic spot called Tanunda Creek. My father and his sisters had known and loved it in their youth and he took us there each year.

At the summit of the hill there was an area of native bush to be passed through, then a short gentle slope to the picnic spot on the banks of a creek. The terrain was open and dotted with gum trees. Dad, who knew everything, could identify them. 'That's a red gum,' he'd say, or 'I think that's a blue gum . . . This looks like a sugar gum.' They all looked the same to me. I marvelled at his knowledge.

Everything had to be carried, so we took only essentials. Food, of

Tanunda Creek, South Australia.

course. There was always plenty of food. The black billy, blackened by years of use and with its own made-to-measure cover of hessian, was almost like a member of the family. The tea that came from it had a distinctive smoky taste, redolent of gum leaves and campfires.

After the long walk we were hungry, so we would collect firewood and boil the billy. Then out came the sandwiches—salmon or egg, with green curling lettuce leaves. There was usually yellow cake topped with slices of apple and sprinkled with sugar and cinnamon and baked to fragrant perfection.

After lunch we played near the creek, scrambling over lichen-covered rocks. There was an unusual type of sand there which when mixed to just the right consistency made a kind of slurry almost like icing for a cake. Dad cut some rushes, constructed the framework for a miniature house and then, with patience and skill, showed us how to drop tiny amounts of the mixture from a cup and so form the walls. I tried—it looked so easy—but to no avail. I finished up with a watery, sandy puddle.

Out came Dad's trusty pocket knife again. More reeds were cut and he began to fashion a water wheel. Deftly he cut slits in the narrow stems and threaded the rushes through so that they were like spokes radiating from the hub. A stronger reed formed the axle. Then two stout forked sticks were driven in on either side of the stream and lo, the water wheel was in motion, to my unutterable delight.

When the shadows began to lengthen, we would pack up and start the homeward trek. First stop was the area of native bush. This was special for us because we knew that in the spring the trees sheltered an abundance of wild flowers. We had our own names for them. There were coffee stars and cat's claw, but the ones we loved most were the native orchids. They came in a variety of colours. In early August there were the sky blue ones, then came the pink ones, followed by the taller purple orchids. The aristocrats were the spider orchids. The white ones clustered like creamy stars under the trees. The green ones were striped with dark red. We prized them greatly.

Arriving home we would fill vases with the spoils of our outing. I have this pleasant image of us returning over the hills towards milking time, carrying our bunches of flowers and singing together with the sun casting long shadows over the grassy slopes.

1940s
Santa's Helper

~

Oho Kaa

Christmas Eve was always a time of excitement for my three brothers, my sister and me. We knew we would get something from Santa Claus but never knew what it might be. All day there was talk about what sorts of things we would like, but in the end we would be quite content with a hankie and comb or some such present. Each of us had our kits and there was always a big fuss to decide where we should hang them: above our heads, or at the foot of the bed, or on the wall near the window? They had to be in a place where Santa would be sure to find them.

Then Mum would call, 'Better get into bed now, Santa has so many places to go to. If he passes our house and you are not asleep, he may miss you altogether.'

That warning was enough for us to get our kits in place, usually at the foot of our beds, and into bed smartly and off to sleep.

One Christmas Eve—I was about seven—I woke up quite late with a bleeding nose. Sitting up in bed with my hand cupped under my nose, I noticed a light on in the kitchen and made my way up the long passage towards it. What a surprise for both my mother and me. There she was with all the presents—a beautiful doll and a smaller soft doll, a small tip truck, a bulldozer and a meccano set, laid out on the kitchen table. There I was with my bloody nose, staring wide-eyed at the unbelievable scene before me.

The interesting thing I learned that evening, besides the fact that our mother was Santa Claus, was that the RSA saw to it that the five of us—and all other children in our situation—would get a Christmas gift until we were fifteen years old.

With my bleeding nose taken care of, Mum asked me to be her helper in parcelling up each present. What a thrill it was for me to hold my very own doll, something I had always secretly wanted, and then to creep into my brothers' bedroom and deposit their gifts into the appropriate kits, knowing full well the joy and excitement for them in the morning. And then into my sister's and mine as well.

Our task over for the night, I hugged my mum. She whispered, 'Goodnight, Santa's helper, let this be our secret'—and so it remained for several years.

1950s
Off to Boarding School
~
Maringi Riddell

Mum died when I was fifteen years old. Cancer of the duodenum, the doctors at the hospital said. I didn't even know what a duodenum was until I studied Human Biology the following year.

Losing my mother was a very painful experience for me. I ached emotionally and physically, and spent much of the time during the following days crying. Sleep would relieve the aching for a while, but when I woke in the mornings, I'd start aching all over again.

My grandmother, who was looking after us at the time, called a whānau hui, and it was decided that we children should move away from home. Perhaps the change of environment would help us get over Mum's death. As a result, my sister Ra, who had stayed at home to nurse Mum during her illness, went off to Gisborne to train as a nurse. I would go to Queen Victoria School in Auckland, and brother Kelly would go to Te Aute College in Hawkes Bay.

I agreed to go because I knew it was for the best. My cousin Heather was going too. It wasn't long before the wheels were in motion. A place at the school was secured, uniforms and gear bought and named, aeroplane tickets reserved, hotel rooms in Auckland booked. It was decided that Auntie Kaa would take me.

The excitement of it all was immense. My first plane trip, and to Auckland. Staying at a hotel, even. I'd never been inside one before. Auckland turned out to be a shock to the system. Miles and miles of concrete roads; skyscrapers; millions of cars; loud noises; unfriendly people, and crowds of them, everywhere.

We stayed at the Central Hotel in Victoria Street, only a few yards away from Queen Street. I remember being in the lift, and a very sophisticated looking man struck up a conversation with me. I felt very uneasy in his presence and was greatly relieved to get out of the lift at my floor. Apart from that one incident, staying at the hotel was everything I imagined it would be—soft lights, petticoat tablecloths, gleaming silverware, linen serviettes, and waiters hovering around serving delicious food. Our rooms were just magnificent, with our own private bathroom and loo, and huge, comfortable beds. And I just loved having clean linen each day. Sheer luxury!

A couple of days later, however, I was plunged back into reality. As our taxi whisked us off to Parnell, I envisaged my new school. It was going to be a two-storeyed brick building, with ivy creeping all over it, nestled at the end of an oak tree lined drive. Imagine my surprise when we pulled up outside a huge wooden building looking more like a haybarn than a residential college. My dismay increased even more when we went inside. There were dark, narrow corridors leading to dingy classrooms and dormitories. But the greatest shock of all was the bathroom. Three baths were standing there in the open—no dividers, no privacy. I was greatly relieved to see some showers at one end with their compartments and curtains. Phew! I decided that it was going to be the showers for me, not the baths. (As it turned out, it was several weeks before I was game enough to have a bath.)

Adjusting to boarding school life was extremely difficult. I was desperately homesick, and yet I didn't know why, because there was no one at home to miss except my grandmother. Most nights I cried myself to sleep. It's a wonder I wasn't called Tangiweto (Crybaby). I don't know how I survived that first term, but I did. When I got home for the May holidays, I announced that I wouldn't be going back to Queen Vic. My grandmother looked at me for what seemed an eternity, and quietly said, 'Me hoki ano koe ka tika, e moko' ('Going back is the right thing to do, my grandchild').

I felt shattered. I knew that I didn't have the courage to disobey her. And yet, by the end of the holidays, I was looking forward to going back. I knew that I was going to be all right.

1930s
Stopping to Look
~
Joyce Harrison

It's fun to be on holiday with Mum and Dad and Auntie in the strange big house with wide windows in this place called St Omer. We are in the Sounds, although there don't seem to be any strange noises. A kind lady hurries around in her kitchen making breakfast, asking what they would like to eat, though she does not quite ask Janne separately. Even the bread tastes different.

The morning's plan is to go for a walk. That would be very different too from the footpaths of Karori. At St Omer it means just wandering anywhere over the hillside. The sun is warming up now, and Janne knows that although she is the youngest, being not quite four, she can easily keep up with the others.

Out through the garden they start, past a few flowers and through several gates. Mum and Dad and Auntie seem to have so much to talk about here, even more than at home, but it is no use trying to follow what they are saying. Janne runs ahead and then drops back. Why come on holiday and then spend all the time talking about other things?

Suddenly she hears a strange sound, a sort of choking, coming from away over on one side. She swings around and comes to a big wire-netting cage. It's a dolls' house with a brown painted roof. There is a mess of mud on the ground and bits of green veges and a chunk of pumpkin. Above all that there's something large and dark and alive. The snorting came from there, as if the thing had a bunged up nose.

The grown-ups go quite close without stopping, but Janne creeps nearer. She starts back. An enormous grey face is staring at her with nasty little eyes. It has a huge nose pressing on the wire, flat and pale and pink at the end. (Has it been sliced off where it should have been much longer?) The flat nostrils quiver sadly. On each side of them are spiky grey and white whiskers, sticking straight out like needles. Its mouth is a rubbery hole. The head goes down to the mud and Janne can see twitchy little ears. She screams after the others, 'What is it? What is it?'

They turn.

'It's just a pig,' they call back, laughing.

'Come and see it,' she demands. They wander over in a dreamy sort of way as if they are still talking to each other silently. They stare politely at the pig.

'Look at its poor nose,' says Janne. 'It must hurt in all that mud. Does it like being so messy?' She must keep talking or they will move on.

No one seems to know. They stare for a bit longer while the pig goes back to its pumpkin. Then they all continue the walk. Nothing else turns up anything like so interesting . . .

On the way back there is a blue hydrangea bush, ever so much bigger than the ones at home. The flower heads lean out like curious faces wanting to be friends. Each one has lots of little eyes and, just underneath, lots of little ears. Janne edges up to the lower ones at eye level, and singles out the nearest flower. She gives it a cool stroke to show that they understand each other.

'When I grow up,' says Janne, 'I'm *always* going to stop and look.'

'Good for you,' says the hydrangea flower. It sounds just like Mum.

1940s
A Winter's Night

~

Heather Williams

It's cold and dark outside, rain peppers the windows and the wind howls around the house, sometimes sending little puffs of smoke back down the chimney, then snatching dancing flames back up again.

It's Sunday night. We are gathered around the fire, chairs pulled close, my sister and I curled up on the sofa in our nighties, ready for bed. Mother sits on one side of the fireplace, her gentle face and golden hair lit by the firelight, her busy fingers stitching a kaleidoscope of colour into a tapestry, darning socks, knitting for us girls or crocheting. Daddy sits opposite with an open book in his hands from which he reads aloud Robbie Burns, Shelley, Keats or Wordsworth or Shakespeare. I love the rhymes and rhythms of the verses and the strange language of Shakespeare's characters. Did people really speak like that?

I'm soon lost in Wordsworth's 'host of dancing daffodils' or Shelley's 'singing still dost soar and soaring ever singest'—magical words that fill my heart with joy and lift my spirit to the sparkling realms of light.

Soon it is time for bed. Reluctantly we leave the warmth of the fire and scamper quickly into our much cooler bedroom where on frosty nights the window panes will be rimed with fantasy shapes left by the crystal ice fairy. Hurriedly we snuggle up under the bed clothes, the kapok mattresses moulded around our bodies all warm and snug and cosy.

We call, 'Come on, Daddy—we're in bed,' and in he'll come to sit on one of our beds and tell us one of our favourite Bible stories—about how the beautiful Queen Esther saved her people or how baby Moses was found in a basket among the rushes or, best of all, about the baby Jesus born in a manger with the animals standing around. Beautiful tales, they warm our hearts and bring a sense of peace and wonder.

Prayers are said, we are kissed goodnight and then lulled to sleep, wrapped in the warmth of the stories, with the sound of the rain still peppering the windows in the darkness of the winter's night and the wind howling about our house.

1940s
The Little Jug

~

Joyce Harrison

It was so strange going to stay with a big family.

At breakfast it was a bit of a squeeze. Shirley, the one nearest to Janne's age, and her little brother David, didn't seem too happy about having to squash up on the wooden bench against the wall; so suddenly, too, with Janne's Mum having to dash off to Christchurch to Grandpa in hospital. If she had been a grown-up visitor Janne supposed she would have had a proper chair like the one John the eldest sat on or even one of the stools used by the twins, Dick and Don. Mr Bruce sat at the end, as he should, but Mrs Bruce didn't sit down at all. She didn't even have a place set. She just bent over the coal range fixing toast and stirring porridge. Janne supposed she ate hers in peace after everyone had gone. Perhaps she even smoked a cigarette? Janne did a little giggle at the cheeky thought.

But what really fascinated her were all the little milk jugs spaced out round the table with the sugar and marmalade. She learnt very smartly, however, when she reached out to the nearest jug for her porridge, that each one had a very definite owner and this one was Shirley's . . . There wasn't one for her. She was to share the big jug that Mr Bruce used for his coffee.

On the way to school Janne asked Shirley why they all had separate jugs. Shirley explained that it was to make sure everyone had a fair share of milk. Next morning Janne made a careful study of those jugs. How could they be fair? They were around the same height but so different in shape. Twelve-year-old John's was pot-bellied with cherries and a long spout like pulling a face with your lower lip. On the other hand Dick's and Don's started narrow at the bottom and widened upwards like arum lilies. There was a daffodil up each side—all a bit sissy for boys but they guarded them just the same. Don's had a chip out of the rim so you knew which was which. It would have been helpful, Janne reflected, if he had had a chip out of his ear too, to tell them apart. The standing-up duck with milk coming out of its beak was of course David's. Shirley's jug was just right for her, a real girl's jug: rounded, and made of twirly glass. Everyone could see all the time exactly how much milk she had left.

That afternoon, Shirley asked Janne what she wanted most of all in the world for when she was grown up. Janne privately thought that to become a grown-up was about as likely to happen as sprouting angel wings and floating around heaven. She was tempted to be silly and say, 'My own little jug,' but instead asked Shirley what *she* wanted, as she was expected to do. Shirley slowly stretched her hands apart.

'A kitten?' Janne guessed, knowing better.

'No, a baby girl.'

'What would you do with it?'

But Shirley was just looking dreamy. David must have been a baby not too long ago, and now he was just boring, the way kittens turned into cats.

Next morning the jugs were once again filled with milk, but there were still only five. Janne thought guiltily of the afternoon recently when she had persuaded Shirley to go hunting for spider's nests and they both arrived home filthy dirty. Perhaps this was the explanation.

That night Janne developed a sore throat and woke with a heavy cold. Trying to hide it proved useless, and by the time the others had left for school she was undressed and back in the huge iron bed, studying the guest room for the first time in daylight. The sun glanced in briefly soon after breakfast but did not look like coming back, though the sky remained a chilly blue through the window. The walls were panelled halfway up with dark timber. The varnished wardrobe doors all along one wall ran right up to the picture rail.

Beside the bed was a little cabinet with a door. Behind that was an enormous potty. (Who could need such a big one?) A pattern of leaves decorated the edge, but it was bigger than any jug. At least the bed was cosy, or the bit of it that Janne had warmed up with a touch of fever.

When Mrs Bruce called in, bringing a book called 'Little Lord F something', she seemed warmer too. Perhaps she liked children best when they were sick, like Shirley longing for babies. Janne thought of her mum saying how some mothers were really fondest of babies, and as each one started to grow up they would have another, and then would look forward to the arrival of their grandchildren. Then there were other mothers who found their children more interesting when they were older and they could talk together.

A clatter of crockery was followed by the arrival of a whole tray of lunch: steaming vegetable soup, hot toast and stewed apple—and, wonder of wonders, milk in her own little jug. And what a special one! Real silver! It must be from the tea-wagon in the dining room.

Janne picked up the jug carefully. It was almost square with a long thin handle that ended in a curl. Across the middle was a groove, and below that it looked as if a comb had been dragged down the side while the silver was still soft. The upper half was shiny, reflecting Janne's red nose and her eyes slanting away round the sides. Though she looked odd in the jug, maybe she wasn't such an obnoxious person after all. She poured the last of the cool milk into her glass—tonight's pudding could take its chances. She snuggled down with poor little Fauntleroy. It was still daytime of course, but, as she confided to him, it would be safe now to go to sleep.

1940s
An Important Decision
~
Jeannette Hunter

Despite the fine weather I stood shivering on the quay. It was packed with people, mostly in family groups: fathers and mothers, babies, grandparents and children. Small suitcases, bags and bundles everywhere. But there was no happy waiting-for-a-holiday-trip atmosphere. The faces of the grown-ups were grim, and the children didn't laugh or run about. This was May 14th, 1940.

The Dutch army was about to surrender to the overwhelming force of the German troops. The royal family had seen the inevitable outcome of the invasion and fled to England four days earlier. Good friends of my parents had phoned to say they were going to IJmuiden, on the North Sea coast, to try to escape to England. Were we going to do the same?

It was a difficult decision to make so suddenly. With the German occupation of our country there would certainly be persecution of Jews, but going away would mean leaving my mother's mother and my father's sisters behind. We agonised over this dilemma for more than an hour, and the outcome was that we should try to save ourselves. As my grandmother was born in Indonesia she was registered there and nobody would know that she was Jewish, so she was safe. My aunts didn't want to come, no matter how much we urged them.

Unlike our friends, we didn't have a car to take us the 25 km to the coast; and as the trains didn't run anymore, Father ordered a taxi to take us to IJmuiden. Mother said, 'Pack only a small bag with things you might need in the next few days, some extra shoes, a warm coat, a clean dress and some undies,' and off we went. I didn't want to look back at our house. What would happen to it and our precious possessions?

When we arrived, a fishing boat was just leaving the harbour, taking our friends to freedom on the other side of the Channel. We could see them waving, but what they were shouting was blown away by the wind. Father went to negotiate with the skipper of the next fishing boat that was being prepared to set sail, but he asked more money than my father had in his pocket. In our hurry we did not have time of course to go to the bank before we left Amsterdam. I saw some of my former classmates totter over the narrow gangplank onto the ship that already looked dangerously overloaded.

'Goodbye Eddy, all the best,' I called when they sailed off. But Eddy never reached England. A German plane bombed the ship only a few miles out of IJmuiden.

After that no skipper wanted to risk his boat or his life. The exodus ceased abruptly. We arrived home frustrated, but also with a feeling of relief to be back where we belonged. It wasn't long before we had to leave home again.

1940s
Home Town Identified
~
Kay Carter

At one time—in my time, that is—the wide main street of Cambridge was lined with trees. But the leaves from their tall spreading branches created a problem for the adjacent buildings, and the roots erupted through the tar seal, so they were removed, except for a few that surround the park at the northern end of Victoria Street. Also gone are many of the shops that were then familiar, and gone with them are the sounds and smells that distinguished them.

When we came to town from our farm at Monavale, some six miles along the road towards Te Awamutu, our parents invariably went to the Farmers Trading Company, where most of their needs could be met. My mother would sit on a high stool in the grocery department and the white- or grey-coated grocer would scurry up and down a tall mobile ladder, assembling the items from her shopping list. There were very few pre-packed goods except for sugar in 70 lb bags or flour in large cotton bags. Other items had to be weighed and bagged on the long, dark-stained waist-high counter.

Recycling was alive and well. The flour sacks were washed, bleached and used for many items such as handkerchiefs and the linings for boys' trousers. Sugar sacks were used for making aprons or pot holders or training material for young embroiderers. My favourite cushion cover had a sugar sack base. I covered it with an embroidery owl sitting on a branch encircled by a full moon.

The two banks did more than provide financial services. They were also the avenue through which new blood entered the town. In later years some members of my family gained employment and met marriage partners in these institutions. When my brother became engaged to a bank employee it had to be kept a secret until the time was right for the bride-to-be to resign. Had the bank heard about it before that time she would have been asked to leave. Certainly no married women were employed in a bank.

Calvert's Drapery was another department store, remembered for its oiled wooden floors, two storeys and two entrances. One entrance was for women's and girlswear and the other for men's and boyswear. The material for my boarding school clothes was bought at Calvert's, and blue velvet for my Sunday best dress for which my grandmother crocheted a Peter Pan collar.

They boasted the latest technology in customer service: the fascinating Lamson vacuum tube which removed the need for on-the-counter cash registers. Purchase docket and cash were placed in a cylinder which was sucked up with the sound of a big metallic intake of breath through a big tube to the cashier on the first floor. We would watch it disappear, and wait until it returned to drop with a swish and a clonk into the wire basket under the trapdoor, complete with change and receipt.

The glass-topped counter displayed scarves, gloves and hankies, etc. to tempt customers and fascinate me. Upstairs the millinery department had hats for every occasion. Each counter throughout the store had a high stool, provided for customer convenience.

Miss Brewster's womenswear and baby shop was a special place. My parents knew the owner, so it was a meeting point for the family. My brother and I waited there after our music lesson at St Peter's Convent, and in my early teens I was happy to cycle the six miles from the farm to Miss Brewster's where I had a school holiday job. Unpacking and pricing boxes of women's lingerie, scarves and hankies and the boxes of tiny frilly baby clothes was the best part of the job.

Miss Lyons' hairdressing salon up the street was redolent of perming solution. Then there were the auction rooms, Howarth's book and toy shop and, further along, the Tudor picture theatre. The auction rooms held many fascinating items—boxes of things which were presumably of use to someone. Our first bicycles came from there, Dad repairing and painting them—always black—before we saw them. I was in my teens before I got my first new bike and then only because I had to cycle each week to boarding school in Hamilton. Amid all the hardware there were chooks for sale in boxes made of light wooden slats wired together. And my brother and I would sell pottles of blackberries there, gathered from the farm.

As the years passed we were sometimes allowed to cycle into the Saturday matinee at the cinema. We stood when *God Save the King* was played before each show—to the accompaniment of Jaffas rolling down the sloping floor, as those who were lucky enough to afford lollies rose to their feet. The first half of the programme would feature a newsreel, a cartoon and the serial, usually a Western. At the end, the announcer would tell us not to miss 'the next exciting episode'—but many times we had to.

As teenagers we looked forward to the Friday night pictures. We walked the circuit: up one side of Victoria Street, over and down the other side, past the Tip Top milk bar and into Duke Street. At Panettiere's fish and chip shop we crossed the road to the forbidden 'Blue Moon', hangout of the milk bar cowboys. Thick malted milkshakes or a spider—creaming soda with ice cream beaten in—were the order of the day. On these walks we would look out for our friends to see if they were going to the pictures and, if we were lucky, we would pair off.

Miss Rippon, who as far back as I can remember was a stooped little old lady, had a small sweet shop, repository of mouthwatering aromas and tantalising coloured treasures. Loose sweets were stored and displayed in rows of big glass jars on the counter and shelves. Apart from Throatees and Vicks cough drops, not many sweets were packaged. We would agonise for ages over how to spend our threepences. The choice seemed endless—smokers, small and pink; conversation sweets, each with its own message; gob stoppers or changing balls, big and mouth filling and either changing colour or delivering chewing gum in the middle. Black balls and brandy balls; long candy sticks, peppermint flavoured and patterned on the outside or down the centre. Licorice straps and LLCs—these small flat oblong sweets were actually for colds, but tasty anyway. Ice creams in penny cones and Eskimo pies rounded off her wares.

From the bookshop Mother collected her *New Zealand Woman's Weekly* until she cancelled her order, considering it to hold too many advertisements. My brother and I could buy comics so long as they were Walt Disney, Superman or Classics. I bought much of my collection of royal family books there. The preference for my brother and father was *Popular Mechanics*.

My family was well known in the district and town, having been among the first settlers there after the Land Wars in the 1860s. One day, returning after many years' absence, I was stopped in the street by someone saying, 'You're Alan Fisher's daughter, aren't you?'

It made me realise I had arrived in my home town!

1940s
Cutting Apricots
~
Mavis Boyd

One of the seasonal activities requiring total family participation always occurred, by happy coincidence, during the long summer holidays. This was when the apricots ripened and were dried and sold to the local cooperative. Usually it was the men who picked the fruit while the women and children would cut it and place the apricot halves on wooden trays to be sun-dried.

The work was monotonous but pleasant, and when the fruit was ripe it was given priority. There was an unquestioned urgency about it, so when Dad said, 'We'll be cutting tomorrow,' we all knew what to do.

We had been trained for this work from early childhood. Dad had invented a cutter for those too young to be trusted with a knife. This consisted of a piece of metal with a sharp-edged V cut out of it and fixed in a stable wooden base. The apricot was held in both hands and rotated, leaving two neat halves.

Anyone skilled with a knife could attain greater speed than a child using a cutter, so we were all pleased when we graduated to using a knife. Speed was important, partly because the fruit should not be allowed to discolour or dry out and partly because we were paid according to individual output. But speed was never as important as accuracy. Dad kept a watchful eye on the quality of our work and was quick to point out any ragged edges or sloppiness. Neat rows of perfectly cut halves was what he wanted to see. Then we could race each other as much as we liked.

In an abundant season we would spend many days sitting in the cutting shed. My mother worked with us, and would exclaim with delight from time to time at some choice specimen of fruit. Dad would check our knives each time he came in with a load of fruit. Out would come the sharpening stone he carried with him and he would work each blade so it was as sharp as possible.

Childhood

The weather was often very hot, but Dad had built an airy shed with a thatched roof so that we could be relatively comfortable. When the day's cutting was finished, the trays of apricots were stacked on to trolleys and wheeled into the sulphur house. Brilliant yellow sulphur was burned and the choking fumes permeated the fruit for several hours so that the apricots would keep their colour. Unsulphured fruit turned black as it dried, so it could not be sold—but it tasted better.

Then for days the trays of fruit were spread out on the drying ground in the hot sun and stacked again each evening to avoid any dew or moisture. Any hint of rain sent us scurrying to the drying ground to stack the trays because the whole process would have been ruined if the half-dried fruit had got wet.

Once the season began the whole process flowed easily. It was a cycle, with picking, cutting and drying going on simultaneously. As we stacked each evening, and laid out the trays each morning, we could observe the various stages of the drying process. The fruit dried, the colour deepened, it shrank in size and left gaps on the pale drying boards.

Apricots drying in the sun, South Australia.

Morning and afternoon tea breaks were highlights. If there was no cake, we would have bread, butter and Vegemite, which in that context tasted especially good.

The early mornings are the times I remember most vividly. Sometimes I would go over to the shed before the others to make an early start and build up a good score. The fruit would be waiting, having been picked the night before. There it was in buckets, cool and firm to the touch, almost luminous in the shadowy corners of the shed, its fragrance filling the air. I loved being there by myself, relishing the peace and quiet that preceded the bustling activity of the day to come.

Those summer days spent cutting apricots coalesce into a blurred but pleasant image of warmth, companionship, singing, storytelling and laughter, and above all a feeling of security. Sharing important work, falling into line unquestioningly with a schedule not of one's choosing—these were all valuable experiences. The loss of these things in a world of automation and labour-saving devices extracts perhaps a greater price than we are prepared to acknowledge. It's difficult to tell. But I know that some of my fondest childhood memories are of those hours spent in the cutting shed more than half a century ago.

1930s
166

~

Shirley Dobbs Signal

From when I was nine until I was thirteen, we lived in an absolutely fascinating house. It was really very tiny and certainly very tatty, but to a child other things are more important. Trees grew all around the small back yard. You could do a Tarzan, swinging from branch to branch around the entire circuit without your feet touching the ground. In the bushy centre of the section there was an incredibly large and very old clump of bamboo, probably infested with spiders and other wildlife—but since we had no consciousness of their presence they impeded us not at all. The interior of this clump made a wonderful cave, and the bamboo canes became spears or whips depending on whether we were marauding tribesmen in Darkest Africa, or pioneers driving their covered wagons across the American prairies. Later, I found a large forked branch of cabbage tree. It became a team of horses. I ran a rope around the forks, placed an old wooden box behind, and drove my team across continents, singing *Roll Along Covered Wagon* to my heart's content.

My singing, however, did not always win hearts. One day I was perched high in the branches of a tree overlooking our boundary fence, giving tongue to an endless hymn to the sun, my mind probably off in the Andes somewhere with the Incas. Like a dash of cold water in the face, the elderly gardener in his vegetable garden next door rudely brought me back to the present. Goaded beyond endurance, he suddenly shouted, 'For goodness' sake, be quiet!' I was quite shocked, and climbed down out of the tree with my feelings totally wounded. Had he no imagination?

There was a back porch, on which I sat on Sunday mornings, shelling peas for the midday dinner. None of the refinements of frozen vegetables! Then the cream had to be whipped, and what a nerve-wracking job that was! If I allowed my attention to wander one miserable second, it seemed, that cream went to butter—and I went to the doghouse!

In the small lounge, known more often in those days as the front room, was the piano. I spent many hours in that place, practising. It was a dark little room, and rather lonely, but I can still see in my mind's eye a frieze around the top of the wallpaper, full of plump yellow peaches against a black background, with splashes of red. I wonder how often my eyes travelled that frieze while my fingers travelled those interminable scales?

It was here that I used to take refuge whenever *Fu Manchu* was broadcast. I found the serial utterly terrifying, and it often sent me rushing into the lounge to hide behind the couch with my fingers in my ears. The opening bars of Sibelius' *Finlandia* introduced the programme, and I still can't hear those ominously portentous chords without a shiver of apprehension.

Our cats loved number 166 too. Apart from all those trees to climb, there was a huge patch of catmint in the garden. The cats would nibble at it and act inebriated. How I used to go into fits of laughter at their drunken antics! Poor things, they didn't know any better, and gosh . . . 'it wash a loverly life . . . hic!'

The little outside washhouse was dreadful—but not to me and my friends. A large old trunk was packed away in there, and inside that trunk was a quantity of old clothes that made marvellous props for dressing up. We each had our favourite outfit, and woe betide anybody who tried to commandeer it except by special and prior arrangement —usually bribery and corruption of the finest order.

There was an old piano case in one corner of the yard. This became the bar of my Wild West saloon. I had a set of old, chipped glasses in which to serve the whiskey. It was my Wild West phase, and I had read all of Clarence E. Mulford's *Bar 20* books, not to mention some of Zane Grey. There were strong silent heroes for you! My favourite toy was a six-shooter my father had found for me. He had to buy special caps for it on his trips to Levin. It gives me great pleasure to recall that fireworksy smell, and the sensation that I could tackle any low-down varmint of a cattle rustler and come out best.

It was a wonderful place to live during those years of active dreaming but by the time I was thirteen I was ready to move on. College loomed, and Tarzan and the Wild West saloon had to move into the back seat. I can't help but feel sorry for today's children, glued to their television sets. They don't have to use their imaginations. What a lot of fun they miss!

1940s
Saved by 'Madeleine'

~

Rachelle Calkoen

In May 1940, after five days of fighting, the Dutch army had to capitulate. As Jews we expected to be arrested immediately and sent to a concentration camp, which was why quite a few of our acquaintances either tried to or *did* commit suicide.

On the taxi ride back home after our abortive attempt to flee from IJmuiden in a fishing boat, my eldest sister and her husband discussed non-stop the least painful way of ending their lives. They concluded that the best way might be to jump out of the third storey window of our house. That was after they had gone through the possibility of cutting their wrists in the bath or taking all sorts of pills, and the effect this would have in the form of stomach cramps and burning pains.

A very depressing journey. At that time I was sixteen going on seventeen. I had heard about concentration camps in Germany and Poland, and knew that people were tortured and starved there and that most of them died. But I had no idea what really happened. The secret of the gas chambers was kept from us till the end of the war and perhaps that was a good thing, for how could one live with that knowledge?

Dora didn't jump out of the window, but she stood on the windowsill, and I was the one who persuaded her to come back into the room and live.

In the first year not much happened, and this gave us a false sense of security. Everybody had to have an identity card, with photo and thumb print, which you were supposed to carry with you at all times. Regulations came out that forbade any mention of the royal family, who had been successful in fleeing to England and Canada. Some people were arrested for anti-German writing or speaking, but on the whole life went on as before. Then at the end of the year all Jewish professors were dismissed from the universities. The students from the oldest university in Leiden staged a massive strike in protest. The punishment was swift and effective—the Germans closed the university. All persons working for the government had to sign an 'Aryan declaration' which effectively meant that neither they, nor their spouse or fiance(e), nor parents or grandparents, had ever belonged to the Jewish community. Almost everybody signed. Not long afterwards, all Jewish teachers were sacked.

Come January, 1941, we began to see signs on cafes, restaurants, museums, picture theatres, swimming pools, tennis courts and so on, forbidding entrance to Jews. The persecution had started in earnest. Night after night there were raids, especially in the Jewish quarters. People were forced into trucks and taken away to the railway station to be transported to concentration camps—not because they had been involved in any anti-German activity, but because they were Jews and had to be eliminated.

This was the time when we had to go to the registry office and get a big 'J' stamped on our personal identity cards. By May 1942 Jews had to wear the yellow Star of David, with a large letter 'J' for 'Jew' in the middle. To show their solidarity a lot of non-Jews wore the Star as well, but if they were found out they were sent to Amersfort, where the Germans had built a concentration camp.

And then in June it was decreed that Jews weren't allowed to use bicycles, trams, trains, taxis or telephones. We were not allowed to visit the homes of non-Jews, and between 8 p.m. and 6 a.m. we had to stay home.

I was walking on the Dam, the large square in front of the royal palace in Amsterdam, when a policeman stopped me. 'Missy,' he said, 'take that Star off. You don't help these people with wearing it, and you could get in trouble over it.' He couldn't believe his eyes when I showed him my identity card with the fat 'J' on it. His amazement came simply because he had no idea what a Jew looked like. The Germans had pasted posters on empty walls all over town with the most hideous and mean-looking pictures and caricatures to warn people about the 'Jewish danger'. When the policeman saw my blond hair and blue eyes, he just knew I couldn't possibly be one of those dreadful people!

Not long after this incident a friend gave me a stolen ID card from someone with the name Margaretha Madeleine Koebergh, who was about my age. He couldn't do anything about the thumb print, but had taken her photo off and put one of me in its place, and falsified the stamp on the photo very professionally, so that I could use the train and disappear from Amsterdam. Later the resistance groups managed to steal a quantity of blank ID cards so that fake cards could be made with corresponding thumb prints and maybe birth dates, and only a false name under the person's photo.

On one occasion I was arrested in a street roundup, and we all had to hand in our identity cards. This was a particularly bad time for me: I had illegal newspapers in my bike bags. One by one we went before the Kommandant. When it was my turn, I was absolutely terrified as he sat there examining my identity card. But I was saved by my choice of fake identity—he loved Madeleine as a name, and had just read a book about a girl in Paris called that. It so happened that I, too, had read the book so we talked for about ten minutes about the story, and then I went free! Better still, he never told his assistant to examine my bike. After this experience I felt much safer with my new card and confidently lived with it for the rest of the war.

1940s
The School Dance

~

Heather Williams

The School Dance—one of the most exciting events of the year!

From the beginning of the May term Friday night dancing lessons were the most popular activity. For this the pupils of the Southland Girls' and Southland Boys' High Schools came together in St Mary's Hall to learn and practise the skills for the great occasion. The ball was to be held in August on the last Saturday of term.

St Mary's Catholic Hall was newly built, and incorporated the most

CHILDHOOD

Heather, ready for the school dance.

modern technology: a sprung floor. You couldn't help but keep in time on that floor. If you got out of step you would receive a sharp reminder when the floor came up to meet you with a jolt. And if you had the misfortune to be sitting out a dance—especially the Gay Gordons—you would be bounced up and down on your seat so much that it was best to disappear to the 'Ladies'.

There was not much choice of material for a ball gown because rationing was still in force, and precious coupons needed to be saved up for a long time in advance. But in no way did this lessen the excitement of choosing a pattern or designing one's own.

Finally the big night arrived, and off we'd go, all decked out in our finery: hair curled, with perhaps flowers or pearls arranged in it, a pearl necklace, white soft leather buttoned court gloves that reached above the elbow and, to complete the ensemble, a little drawstring handbag made, perhaps, from the same material as the gown. The handbag contained a handkerchief, lipstick (if that were allowed) and a pencil to mark one's 'card'.

Some girls were escorted by boyfriends who would present them with a corsage before they arrived. Most of us went unescorted, and we'd assemble on one side of the hall, chattering excitedly and admiring each other's gowns. The boys gathered on the other side of the hall looking sheepishly awkward but very handsome in black dinner suits, white shirts, black bow ties and, most importantly, white cotton gloves—worn so that their sweaty hands might not stain the girls' gowns.

On arrival we were given a programme, a small white card with a numbered list of the dances the band would play during the evening and a space against each for the name of the boy with whom we would dance for that number.

The air of excitement increased as the band began tuning up: a violin, piano, cello, double bass, drums, possibly a saxophone or an accordion, usually an eight-piece ensemble. From across the hall the boys and girls surveyed each other, covertly of course but with hearts aflutter, until the time came to fill in the programmes. Etiquette demanded that, if a girl were escorted, the first, last and supper waltzes were reserved for her partner. It was considered impolite to have more than three dances with the same boy, so there was anticipation, and hope, that a girl's programme would be filled.

One of the most popular dances was the Monte Carlo. The hall was divided into four—the suits in a pack of cards. Everyone danced until the music stopped, when the Master of Ceremonies would offer a pack of cards to a couple to 'cut'—if the displayed card were hearts then all the couples in that quarter of the hall would leave the floor. This continued until there was only one couple left on the floor. They were the 'winners' and were rewarded with a small prize. Other favourite novelty dances of similar style were the Lucky Spot and the Statue Waltz.

The ball always finished with the singing of 'Auld Lang Syne' at half past eleven, so we could be home by midnight. Were we expected to be like Cinderella, our gowns suddenly turning to rags?

Reluctantly we would leave the bright lights and the evening's gaiety, as parents arrived to take us home. Still agog with the experience, which we eagerly described—reliving each dance in the process—we made our way home. There we reluctantly removed our crumpled gowns, but not before one last twirl and primp in front of the mirror. Necklace removed, shoes kicked off, and into bed, perchance to dream . . .

1950s
Christmas at Mafeking
~
Maringi Riddell

Christmas at Mafeking was an exciting time, and preparing for the hākari was, on the whole, great fun—making the stuffing for the chooks, burning the sugar for the boiled puddings and then watching Auntie Kaa up to her elbows mixing the brown concoction. In would go the sixpences and threepenny bits. I loved to help her tie up the puddings in the flourbag cloths, and feel their rounded, warm bottoms.

Gathering wood for the hāngi, washing the sacks, digging up the stones, and so on, was done days beforehand.

What I hated about the Christmas preparations was the killing of the animals. With no men in our household, Uncle Pitau would come over to kill the pig, and of course we had to help out. My job was to hold the bucket to catch the blood as it spurted out from where the pig had been stabbed. It would be squealing and struggling something dreadful and it was difficult to hold the bucket in the right position, especially with my eyes half-closed.

'Watch what you're doing,' my uncle would yell.

It was important to catch as much blood as possible, you see, to make the blood puddings.

Mum's job was to 'do' the chooks, and usually we needed half a dozen. My brother Kelly would race around the pen catching them, and then present them to Mum to have their heads chopped off. You could tell by her body language that she hated doing that. Often the chooks would run around the back yard with their heads almost severed. I'd make sure that I was perched up high on the woodpile so that they couldn't get anywhere near me. When they eventually died, we all shared in the work of plucking and gutting. I made sure that I was one of the pluckers. Nanny Waioeka and Mum usually did the gutting. Yuck!

Isn't it amazing that after all this blood and guts, I still enjoyed my Christmas dinner?

1930s
Faces
~
Joyce Harrison

Janne was to become well acquainted with Mr Sergeant the optician. She progressively grew up the buttons of his tubby waistcoat and learnt to respond to his jolly smile. By the time he began frowning instead—at her proposal to take driving lessons—she was able to look down on the top of his balding head.

No visit was so memorable, however, as the occasion on which, as a three-year-old, she was taken to collect her first pair of glasses.

Mr Sergeant's little passageway and high wooden counter were already familiar. So was the dim room behind, from which he now appeared, carrying a little box. As he bent down to her, he made it jump open and up sprang a huge ant made of glass. He gently pushed her hair back from the sides of her face, just as if he knew her properly, and looped the springy legs behind her ears. Little feet settled one each side of her nose.

In that moment bright squiggles in yellows and browns leapt up in the varnished surface of the counter beside her. Delightedly she beamed up at Mr Sergeant who now had proper eyes and a mouth, even standing up, and a happy pink smile. She swung round to her mother, alongside. She too now had a clear face, but to Janne's surprise there wasn't any smile at all. She rubbed her mother's skirt urgently, straining her face up to try to see what had happened, but the face above still went on looking sad.

Janne glanced back and forth at the two faces. Why was one happy, the other not? she puzzled, but even the new glasses could not see any answer to that.

1930s
Rebellion
~
Shirley Dobbs Signal

Our class has been driven beyond endurance by its new teacher. Today we are On Strike. This is unheard of. It's 1939 and strikes are not that common, even on the industrial scene. But we are in school, and we are only in Standard Five. We are terrified about the possible consequences of our actions but determined, each boy and girl, to stick it out.

The headmaster is summoned. He looks over and around us, gravely. 'Now, what's this all about?'

Poor Miss Fowler stands to one side, face flushed deep crimson. There is a deafening silence. Now the crunch has suddenly come, and not one of us is going to risk a neck.

Mr Banks looks around the room again. Then, horrors! He turns to me. 'Shirley. You tell me one thing that's upsetting you all.'

I feel horribly like a butterfly on a pin, and I'm not chloroformed either. I haven't yet learned about the frantic, silent plea to 'Above' for help. 'Above' helps me anyway.

'Perhaps, Miss Fowler,' I hear myself stammering, 'you could stop telling us about how much better than us your last class was . . .'

It proves to be the key that unlocks all the tongues, some of them far braver, more forthright, than mine. Mr Banks is a coolheaded and wise arbitrator. By the end of the session Miss Fowler's face is nearer a normal colour, and the class is headed towards a good and stable relationship with their teacher. There are no repercussions.

And I can wriggle off my pin!

1940s
The Farm Holiday

~

Shirley Dobbs Signal

Her mother had an important war job, so my best friend had to go away for the school holidays. Not that she minded. She spent the vacation on a farm in Otaki. Twice I went with her. The second time, my parents came up to visit—they had not seen the place before. Wellington to Otaki was a sizable trip in the early war years, and they had taken Mrs Gray's word for the suitability of the farm.

They didn't say much then—but that was the last time I was allowed to stay there. Well, maybe it wasn't your top-notch clean sparkling resort . . . maybe there were a few hundred more blowflies than were usually found in a farm kitchen . . . maybe the tin shed we slept in out back was not entirely draught- and rain-proof and left a little to be desired in security and cleanliness . . . But then, the possums made a delightfully scary noise on the roof at night. And nobody checked to see whether we were going to sleep or not. Parents were so picky about unimportant things!

I learned to live during those farm holidays. We were chased by a bull one day, and I think we were probably lucky to escape with our lives—but I was thirteen, and could hardly wait to get back to the hut and write: 'Dear Diary, today I was chased by a bull! What is this fatal fascination I exert over the entire male sex!' My wittiness almost overwhelmed me, as it did my friend, who was constructing a similar diary entry. We giggled halfway through the night, and felt incredibly sophisticated.

We often went to the rail bridge swimming hole. On one occasion the river was running high—it had rained quite heavily the night before. Six or seven of us dived in and battled the current, which was faster than usual. I didn't battle too well, and was suddenly swept off downriver, coming up against a bridge pylon, where I found myself instantly tipped upside down, pinned and powerless in the grip of the current, head way down underwater against the concrete. Talk about panic. I think it was the panic which saved me. I can't think what else gave me the sudden superhuman burst of strength which shot me upright again. Oh, the bliss of that first gulp of air!

I made my shaky way back to the others to find that no one had even noticed that I was missing. That's how fast it all happened. It was a little sobering to realise how close I'd come to oblivion.

There was an even more sobering experience later in the holiday. The farmer woke us this morning at four thirty, before dawn. We climbed blearily into our clothes (no stupid sissy nonsense about washing) and followed our noses to the kitchen. Great heaping plates of bacon and eggs, tomatoes and fried bread waited there, to stock us up with energy for the day that lay ahead. We were going to help the farmer burn off scrub on the foothills, so there would be more pasture for the sheep. It was special, pottering off down the paddocks, the dawn sky flushed above us and the larks already too high to see, but not too high to hear.

Thirteen-year-olds are not, in the main, noted for sense, and I find it hard to believe that we were given burning brands, and turned loose in the scrub. However, mature reflection brings the realisation that thirteen-year-old girls are noted for giggling silliness, and maybe we had driven the farmer to some dark point of No Return . . .

Whatever, we had a rare time. Nero couldn't have enjoyed himself any more torching Rome! Half the hillside was ablaze, and nothing more to do except control it. I looked round for the others. I couldn't see them. I couldn't see anything. I had fired so well that all around me was a high wall of flames, with no gaps at all. There I was, in the middle of a ring of fire, just like in a circus! Again, blind panic came to my aid. Without stopping to consider the consequences, I charged at the fiery barrier and, just like the circus horse, leaped straight through the flames. And, also just like the circus horse, came out safe and totally unsinged. The Valkyries weren't in it!

But I can't say I was unfazed by the experience. I slunk off down the hill to wait at its foot for the others. I'd about had my fill of narrow escapes for one holiday. I lay on my back in the long grass relaxing and chewing a stalk and tried to find the lark who was singing his heart out above me. In this reflective mood I wondered whether God still had a few more things He wanted me to do in this life . . .

1940s
Home to School
~
Oho Kaa

We had moved back to our grandad's house before the 1943 school year was through, but our mother wanted the four of us to continue at the Tikitiki Native School, which was six miles away, until the year ended. She said we could attend Rangitukia Native School, the local one three miles away, the following year.

Because of this we had to rise early each Monday morning to catch the cream cart. The cream cart took us as far as Rangitukia school. Then our uncle, who drove the cream truck, drove us to Tikitiki school on his way to the Ruatoria cream factory. We stayed with our aunt and uncle in Tikitiki till Friday afternoon, when we caught the bus back to Rangitukia and walked the three miles home.

We always got to the cream stand before the cart arrived. The driver, Rutene, was a small yet strong man, and he would expertly swivel the heavy cream cans, arranging them so that the load was evenly balanced. Then he would give us a helping hand to get up from the ground to the high step-up on to the cart. We sat snug in the space he had left for us between the cans. He always sat on the side rail of the cart. A slight tap on the horse's back with his long rein and we were jolting merrily along. I loved the crunching, crackling sound as tiny stones went flying from the huge revolving wheels. Rutene loved to whistle as we rolled along, stopping here and there to pick up the cans from the stands.

Sometimes he would let my older brother hold the reins and, as my brother became more confident, he was able to drive the cart close enough to the stands for Rutene to heave the cans of cream on to the cart, and then drive on again.

One such morning, when the last can had been collected, Rutene sat on a can at the back of the cart and said, 'Go on boy, let's go!' He handed the reins to my brother who immediately slapped them on the horse's back. He gave her such a fright that she bolted helter skelter down the stony road.

Rutene was tossed overboard. We hung on for dear life as we looked back at him waving his arms and trying to run. He was left further and further behind. My brother was pulling as hard as he could on the reins and yelling, 'Whoa! Whoa!' On we sped and the school was looming up. We could see the older boys dashing out on to the road waving their arms to try and slow the horse down. The horse raced straight for them and they were forced to jump out of the way.

My brother pulled hard on the right rein as we neared the corner, forcing the horse to turn and run straight up to the shop fence. The sudden stop caused a few cream cans to topple on to us. We weren't hurt too much but the locals insisted on carrying us all to the house nearby while they rang our mother. The kind elderly couple that lived there gave us hot milk to drink from the open fireplace, and kept asking us if we were all right. A concerned Rutene soon arrived, followed by our mother.

Needless to say, we never got to school that day.

1940s
Request From Egypt

~

Lesley Ferguson

The house was glowing with welcome, warm and fresh. There was a pot pourri of smells—freesias, polishing oil and roasting beef. Floors were oiled, the wooden doors gleamed with the patina that only comes with oil and elbow grease, and the old Indian carpet had been

Lesley's father, Fen, aboard the troopship.

Lesley's mother, Enid.

freshened—its cream pile standing in tufts which showed off the richly coloured geometric pattern.

Two wall-lights flushed the walls and ceiling beams above the fire, and an unusual camel's bladder lamp glowed under its pleated shade in the corner.

The brown and cream tones of the room spoke solidity, permanence, and comfort. The smooth dark beams, the fading long brown velvet curtains, drawn to shut out the night (and the window seat), the oiled timbers, the bookshelves each side of the fire, Mother's woodland picture, grandfather Hall's sword candlestick—these were at the welcoming heart of our home.

Mouthwatering smells wafted down the dark passage from the theatre of operations. The kitchen showed Mother's quiet flair for organisation. The dining room was then in the sun porch adjoining the sitting room, a long way from the kitchen. It was match-lined, and just big enough for table, chairs and book cases. Yellow curtains were pulled around the folding-out Whitney windows, and it looked quite formal in its tidy preparedness.

If only Father could have been there to share it, and if only we hadn't been sent to bed . . .

From a tent in the desert Father had written home that his colonel was to visit New Zealand. 'Would Mother entertain him with the usual well-cooked, well-chosen, well-served meal with fine company? In fact, he had promised the colonel already!' She understood the humour of his wording, but privately snorted, 'Well chosen, indeed!' A soldier's pay was a limiting factor, but Mother was used to careful planning, so an occasion such as this was just another challenge.

By the time Colonel Campling put his polished feet on our polished front porch tiles, all was perfection. Slim, nervously calm, Mother was wearing her best black floral crepe dress which fitted so gracefully—a dress that would have been fashionable fifty years later.

The colonel was brought into the warmth and light. Mother's two most elegant friends had arrived already. A Swedish couple, Sixten and Lisa, were indeed fine company—elegant, handsome, and entertaining. It goes without saying that everyone was charming.

Next morning we couldn't wait to hear what had happened, and asked mother what the colonel was like. 'Everything was very correct,' she said happily, 'but the real success of the evening came during dinner. Everyone wanted second helpings when asked and I was so busy with the conversation and the serving that I didn't concentrate properly. I couldn't work out why they were suddenly silent and staring—then I realised. In my nervousness I had forgotten to serve Lisa and Sixten, and was tucking into the colonel's serving, on his plate! That really broke the ice! Now I'll have to write to Dad about the well-served meal!'

1940s
Diary Revisited
~
Shirley Dobbs Signal

The impressions of a sixteen-year-old poured out in her diary . . .

June 6th 1944
The Allied Supreme Command under General Eisenhower.
Communique No 1:

'Allied naval forces, strongly supported by Allied air forces, are landing troops on the French coast.'
Oh God, please have them in your safe keeping.

The news came through first in the 6.15 news, when the announcer reported that the German High Command was saying that Anglo-American parachutists had landed in the Seine estuary. We were wildly excited. If it had been merely a rumour spread to confuse the French and us, the BBC would never have broadcast it to the world.

Uh-oh, they've just said, 'Ladies and Gentlemen, we hope shortly to broadcast another news flash in the voice of General Eisenhower.'

I'm hanging over the wireless with bated breath. It would be tremendously exciting news in the normal course of events, but coming the day after we entered Rome—here's General Eisenhower.

Oh, the news is marvellous. We've been waiting so long for it. How wonderful it must be for the people in the occupied countries. Soon they'll be occupied in another sense. I'm feeling intensely patriotic, but I wish I had more than just a guinea in my National Savings account . . .

Mum is out, she's missing all the excitement of not being able to stir from the wireless set for fear of missing a news flash. It seems too good to be true. It was so wonderful about Rome—we had the Union Jack flying all day at school, and bells were rung, and whistles and sirens went off at noon. The noise was great.

Rome was a symbol, the Germans said we should never take Rome. We did. Then, too, Rome is the first capital we have taken in the struggle for Europe. And what a capital! It hasn't been taken since the Gaulish invasion, and that was something BC! Hannibal couldn't take it, but Alexander has.

And now we have landed in France! There is the most thundering English music on the wireless.

Now they are rebroadcasting Communique No 1! ' . . . began landing Allied armies this morning on the northern coast of France . . . '

All evening the BBC has been broadcasting to Europe. King Haakon of Norway, the Prime Minister of the Netherlands, the Prime Minister of Belgium, and we're expecting a message to the French people from General de Gaulle, who has just landed in England.

'The watchwords we send you are courage, unity and

patience.' That was the conclusion of the Belgian Prime Minister's speech.

'At nine p.m. His Majesty the King will broadcast to his people.'

At twenty-eight minutes past ten this morning the first communique was issued. Oh dear, I have writer's cramp. Oh, I'm so excited, but I'm very glad that I'm too young to have a sweetheart or a husband in the thick of the invasion.

God be with every woman's son, with all the sweethearts, husbands, fathers, brothers . . .

A report from the Supreme Command says we're landing in Normandy . . .

The entry finishes there. The outcome is well known, as are the years of struggle and heartbreak yet to come—the cost in human suffering and disruption of lives too vast to ever be counted.

The memory of that day, when the tide at last began to turn, remains one of the most exciting memories in my life. History in the making, and however tiny and unimportant, I was privileged to be a participant.

Even my children respect this memory!

1940s
The Chase

~

Heather Williams

'Squawk! Squawk! Squawk!' screamed the frightened rooster as it fled in terror round the wood pile, through the orchard, and round again, half flying, half running, this way, that way, trying to escape capture by two girls calling raucously, with murderous intent, 'Quick, catch him! Hurry up! This way!'

Our housekeeper had no meat to cook for the evening meal so Grandpa said there was a rooster in the yard which she could have, and my sister, always more adventurous than me, volunteered to catch and kill it—with my help, of course.

I wanted nothing to do with it as I didn't like feathers much. If life seemed rather dull and she wished to stir up a bit of fun my sister would tease me by chasing me with a feather. Fun for her, maybe. I had a different view.

Grandpa pointed out the doomed bird and Jocelyn made a grab for it and missed. She had decided that I would hold the wretched bird by its legs while she used Grandpa's big wood axe to chop off its head but, as Mrs Beeton would say, 'First catch your rooster.' It seemed to sense its fate, for with a little hop and a squawk it was off. The chase grew more and more frantic.

After much chasing and squawking, yelling and screaming, the wretched bird could run no more and stood exhausted, gasping for breath. Jocelyn quickly seized it by the neck and carried it off to the wood block in triumph.

'Here you are, Heddy. Don't be a silly, hold its legs and don't let go till I say.'

Reluctantly I did as I was told and held the hapless wriggling bird by the legs as tightly as I could, hating the feel of the struggling feet beneath my hands. I turned my head away. I could not bear to witness the awful deed. My sister had trouble deciding when to strike, as the terrified creature kept lifting its head from the block—hoping to give one last, desperate strangled squawk before the axe fell—but to no avail. Down came the axe! Thud!

Immediately I released my grip, but alas the foul deed was not completed. At once the rooster got up and ran for dear life in a sort of sideways gait with its head half off. The chase began all over again, but thankfully not so long and the bird was dispatched with another, more accurate, blow of the axe.

If the rooster's ordeal was over, mine was not. Jocelyn cut off its legs and chased me with a twitching foot, which operated by pulling on the tendon.

I've no idea who plucked the wretched bird. It was 'as tough as old boots', the family said. I couldn't bear to eat it—all I could think of was the poor thing running around with its head half off.

1940s
Rabbits
~
Kay Carter

If you were as lucky as I, and brought up on a farm, I wonder if you ever went hunting for baby rabbits?

It was a weekend in spring, or perhaps during the Christmas school holidays, when four of us aged from twelve down to eight, two cousins, my brother and I, went off armed with a spade on such an expedition. We would probably have been told by one of our fathers where to look, or we might have found a burrow on a previous exploration of our farm.

Perhaps we went looking on the side of a big grassy depression we called the Whare—one of many found in the fields, dating from long before the Land Wars—where we once found several grey stone axe heads when exploring and digging out a rabbit burrow. We had been very delighted with our find, and our Australian farmhand was very keen on them. Our parents told us that we would be sorry later if we let him have them, but since we had found them we were given the responsibility of making our own decision. Our parents were right, although it took a number of years before we recognised the importance and historic value of our find.

When rabbiting, we looked for fresh earth that had been dug out indicating the hole had been deepened overnight, and fresh droppings at one side, showing its recent use. After checking around to make sure there was no escape hole nearby we would begin to dig.

We did not have to go too far before we started to find straw and then fur. The most adventurous of us, probably Peter because he was the eldest, would put his arm into the hole to feel how much further we had to dig or maybe he even found the pad of warm fur pulled from the mother's body, which lined the nest.

And then the babies were all pulled out. If they were less than three weeks old they were like little pink rats, eyes closed and no fur, but if they were older they were real baby rabbits. A black one might be taken home as a pet, but if they were ordinary rabbits we would take them out, hold them by the back feet and bash their heads against the back of the spade. We were farmers' children after all.

1930s
Rural Remembrance

~

Heather Williams

The holidays we spent on our grandparents' farm just a few miles from Ashhurst, near Palmerston North, were wonderful. During the war years we lived there for a while.

Childhood

Many a day we spent out working—perhaps trying to work would be a better phrase, especially when we were quite young. That time-honoured phrase, 'If you can't be a help don't be a hindrance', would encourage us to renew our efforts to please, but sometimes it was better to go and play our own games.

We followed our bachelor uncles around like puppies, clumping along behind them clad in their discarded gumboots, in summer enveloped in their cast-off long-sleeved shirts to protect us from the sun and in winter swallowed up in outsize oilskins.

Over the fields we'd go to help mend fences or ride in the grumbling bumpy old dray drawn by Jock or Prince. Sometimes we were allowed to perch on the backs of these enormous old draught horses, our legs spread wide and barely able to stretch more than a few inches down their sides. That was a real treat. Later it was the roaring tractor with immense spiked steel wheels that left deep angular holes in the soft earth.

We'd always be there to help bring the cows in for milking. Our nostrils were filled with the odour of milk and dust as they slowly,

Heather's grandparents at Waiwiri, near Ashhurst, setting off for Palmerston North.

Haymaking at Waiwiri, near Ashhurst.

unhurriedly mooched along in the hot dusty haze. They didn't need much help as they knew exactly when to come in and where to go. Occasionally the dogs, Pat or Bob, would run along behind and give a sharp bark just to remind them to keep moving.

In the spring there were the little calves to feed once they'd been separated from their possessive mothers. The calves were always in a great hurry, pushing and shoving and butting each other to be first in to their special bail with a bucket of milk ready to gulp down. Quite a stampede in fact. Afterwards they liked to suck our fingers.

Lambing was an especially busy but exciting time, going around the sheep to see the cute little lambs still yellow from birth and so quickly, shakily, rockingly, staggering to their feet under their mother's watchful eye. So soon they'd be wagging their tails and nudging mother for a feed. Within weeks it would be time for the lambs to lose their happily wagging tails. They would then be separated from their source of food and security for a few hours on docking day, but afterwards, amid sniffing and bleating and hectic milling around, the lambs and ewes would be reunited and would trot off to a quiet corner of the field to resume their leisurely routine.

Childhood

Summer! Ah, the hot dreamy days of summer, long golden evenings filled with birdsong, the skylarks soaring, soaring. How I loved those evenings working in the hayfield raking the back cut away from the fence ready for sweeping in the sweet smelling hay in the morning. The skylarks soaring and soaring up and up into invisibility with only silver droplets of song to tell they were there at all, an outpouring of joy for the day now sliding into deep velvet quietness.

Summer was the time also when the weaned and fattened lambs would be brought into the yards for the 'fatbuyer' to select and mark with blue raddle those he felt were ready to be sent to the meatworks. The remainder were returned to the fields to fatten up for another six weeks or so.

This was also the time for haymaking, when men from neighbouring farms all came to help. Draught horses were used to pull a variety of machines, first the mower to cut the hay, then a few days later the rake to form the hay into rows to be swept in by yet another machine to the base of the haystack, where two or three men would be arranging great forks full of hay into a square or oblong shape. Two or three men would throw heavy forks of hay up to the men on top. A labour-intensive and exhausting exercise, all day in the heat. Now the whole job is done by one machine, forming the hay into bales or rolling and wrapping it in plastic like outsize balls.

Autumn . . . It's up early in the fresh crispness of the morning and out across the dewy fields in search of mushrooms for breakfast. Oh, the excitement of finding fairy rings of snowy white buttons among the grass. I imagined fairies circling them in dance.

Home again with full basins to the warm, inviting kitchen where delicious hot porridge simmered on the silvered woodburning stove, the pan with thick rashers of bacon already sizzling waiting for the peeled mushrooms to be gently laid beside them. Mmm! I can still smell the aroma.

Autumn was also the time to harvest the wheat standing tall and golden in the sunlight. The big clanking harvester would arrive and spit out sheaves of wheat all nicely tied with wire and then it was our job, my sister's and mine, to collect the sheaves, about ten or twelve at a time, and stack them into stooks—tentlike shapes—so they could dry thoroughly before another machine came and beat the seed out into sacks ready for the mill.

This job we didn't really enjoy very much, for in spite of wearing longsleeved shirts our arms always got scratched and sore. But the job had to be done. Today one big machine does the lot.

And so to winter when on wet days we'd go over to the big brown red-roofed barn where sacks of superphosphate were stored. There the empty sacks would be opened out and we'd sew them together side by side with great hooked needles and thick brown string to make them into covers for the haystacks in the summer. It was warm in the barn with the wind howling around and the rain pelting the roof. A good theatrical atmosphere for a Hollywood movie!

At the end of the day it was back over the fields, sloshing through the long wet grass, wind and rain whipping our faces, to the warmth and dryness of the welcoming kitchen, hot drinks and food.

1930s
Trespassing
~
Joyce Harrison

'Come and see what's on Mrs Oliphant's lawn,' Skip shouted. Janne hesitated. She wasn't really supposed to play with Skip and Tommy Hooker, even though she'd soon be starting school and they'd be there. It was not exactly that she wasn't allowed, but it was better not to. Just in case . . . in case what?

'Come on, or it will get away.'

That did it. She ran across the road and they went off to Mrs Oliphant's place. Janne didn't ever go to her place either. She, Mrs Oliphant, was a real lady who always came out her *front* door, all dressed up with no time to waste as she tippy-toed on her high heels down the road to the bus stop. There was a round window in the top half of her front door, with fancy coloured glass, not like anyone else's in their street. She also had a roughcast concrete fence painted white, with a beautiful iron gate, which Janne had never looked at close-up before. Then there was lawn sloping up towards the house.

'Did Mrs Oliphant say we could?'

'Yes, of course. She doesn't mind. She *wants* us to see it.'

Janne stopped again. She really did want to believe this; but just because Mrs Oliphant lived next door to the Hookers' place didn't mean she would ever want Skip and Tommy to go tearing round her garden—and bring half the neighbourhood with them.

Skip snapped open the pretty gate as if he did it every day and Janne tiptoed up behind them. By the time she caught up they were squatting on the grass, staring down at it. This seemed all right so she crouched down too; but she kept an eye on the round window all the same.

'Where?' she asked, and then she saw it: a long brown twig that seemed to be alive, a bit up off the ground, with a whole lot of skinny legs and elbows. It was swaying from side to side as if it were just going to sleep, or just waking up.

'What is it?' she whispered.

'A stick insect,' said Tommy, as if he knew all about them and he and Mrs Oliphant owned this one between them. He even gave it a prod. The stick insect stopped swaying. They went on staring, waiting for something else to happen.

'Let's take it home,' said Skip.

Janne gasped; but just then something else happened. The round window seemed to close up. The door opened, and there stood Mrs Oliphant, not at all dressed up. She actually had on big fluffy old slippers. She must be really furious to come out looking like that.

'What do you children think you're doing?' she roared.

'It's a stick insect,' began Skip and then stopped.

'How dare you children come trespassing in other people's gardens. Just get out and go home. It's *my* stick insect. I want it left right there.'

Now she was looking at Janne. Janne supposed she should say something. She didn't seem to belong anywhere.

They ran down the bank together and jumped over the stupid fence. Janne half expected Skip to start singing out 'Silly ol' Mrs Ole!' but he didn't. Tommy was muttering, 'What does she want a stick insect for anyway?' and then, 'I bet she didn't even know it was there.'

Janne quite agreed. She belonged with them—for today.

1940s
Life at St Joseph's Māori Girls' College

~

Oho Kaa

I began to learn about making decisions for myself and organising my own life while at St Joseph's College. The nuns taught some very basic and important skills: who I was, how to behave as a young woman, how to get on with others, and always to do the best I could. The motto, *T o mahi katoa mahia'* which means 'Whatever you do, do', has been an anchor for me through life.

A normal day at St Joseph's began at six in the morning when the rising bell woke us all. In twenty minutes we were expected to be washed, dressed, beds made and downstairs ready to go to chapel. The prefects saw to it that there was no dawdling.

The chapel was a sanctuary for all of us. We were able to go there whenever we felt unhappy or needed to be alone, or just for a quiet prayer. I loved taking part with the girls' natural harmony as they sang the hymns and responses to the various intercessions. These were conducted in English, Latin and Māori. I learnt about the Stations of the Cross, the Rosary, the Saints and so much more.

After chapel, where communion was the order of the day for the Catholics, the one hundred and twenty girls lined the walls of the corridor outside the dining room for morning prayers.

Breakfast consisted of a bowl of porridge, three pieces of toast and a teaspoon of butter. We soon learnt to save most of the butter for the last piece of toast, so that we could really taste it. A cup of tea washed it all down. In spite of three substantial meals a day I always seemed to be hungry.

Each table sat seven girls and a prefect who was in charge. Each Friday, after breakfast, a special light green vase with a rose in it was placed on the table that had the cleanest and whitest tablecloth for the week. The prefect would be on to any girl who accidentally spilt a morsel on the cloth. Many a time someone would be using a bowl of warm soapy water to clean up the spills. The table that held the vase for the week was always the first to leave after every meal. It was very competitive.

We were also taught to eat everything that was placed in front of us. One particular dish that nobody on our table cared for was leeks in white sauce. Our prefect sent the bowl around, but because she did not take any none of us did either. We moved out after that particular lunch with that bowl of leeks still sitting on the table. To our surprise, not even ten minutes later, the eight of us were called back. There on a saucer in each place sat the leeks and a spoon. The sister in charge told us to sit down and eat, with a stiff word never to do that again, and how grateful we should be that we had food to eat, and so on. We shamefacedly ate our share in silence. Then, just as we had escaped outside, we stared unbelievingly as our prefect rushed out and spat all her leeks down the outside drain. She had stuffed them in her mouth but not swallowed them.

After breakfast there were duties. These included the cleaning of showers, face basins, dormitories, corridors, drains, classrooms, dishes, kitchen and porches. Each group of girls had set tasks week by week which were inspected and signed off by a prefect each day. If the prefect was not satisfied, and the job in question was not done again, that person received a black mark. Once a week anyone with a black mark had to stand up in front of the whole school and receive a telling-off. Woe betide those who got two black marks in a row.

Classes began at eight thirty and finished at seven at night from Monday to Friday. There were morning and afternoon breaks as well as an hour for lunch. All classes started with religious instructions then it was the three R's, followed by Māori, English, biology, homecraft and clothing. The nuns were devoted teachers and very caring. We were reminded that we were there at our parents' expense and that we were to put our best foot forward, whatever we tackled. We had exams, and parents were well informed about our achievements. Extra curricula activities included Māori speech competitions, sport and marching. Piano lessons were offered twice a week. I had my fingers slapped for jazzing up the pieces once I had learnt them off by heart.

I loved the weekends. Only on Saturday were we allowed to wear dresses and sandals. This was also washing day. Tablecloths, sheets, pillowslips, towels and white blouses were all boiled in huge coppers, which the girls took turns to boil up. There were big poles to lift out the washing, which was then put through a mangle to squeeze out the excess water, then out on the line it went. At the end of the day the girl on duty would collect, fold, mangle or iron the clothes. Each girl washed her own personal garments.

Saturday was sports and marching day. We played nine-a-side basketball against Hukarere Girls' College and Napier Girls' High. It was very competitive, and our hardest games were always against the Hukarere girls.

Marching to the rhythmic beat of our own drummers was another highlight. We often displayed our marching skills as far away as Palmerston North. Every girl, with no exceptions, took part in the marching squads, which were ranked by height. Since the shortest girls were in our squad, we were called the Midgets.

Saturday evening was social night. The girls who could play by ear played the piano for two hours, much to everyone's delight. Girls danced foxtrots, waltzes, the Gay Gordons, larinka, jitterbug—in fact someone always knew just what to do, whatever the pianist played.

On Sundays we wore our costumes, silk stockings and Panama hats to church. Sometimes we joined the local church service in Taradale. The people liked to hear the girls sing, and for us it was a joy to take part. On these occasions we were able to go for a walk and see the shops in Taradale. It was compulsory on Sunday to write letters home. No penfriends were allowed, but there were times when some of us sneaked letters out. The nuns read our letters before they were sent. They also read all incoming mail.

For me, the best part of Sunday was lunch. It was the only meal I looked forward to. It was very special, simply because it tasted just like the roast dinners we had at home. We had roast meat, potatoes and vegetables followed by steamed pudding, custard and ice cream, which was just out of this world. It was a meal all the girls looked forward to. The rest of the day was spent quietly reading, studying, mending or relaxing.

June was the only holiday we had for the year, so there was always great excitement as the time approached. We raved on about the things we missed most of all about home and how we were going to make up for it in our four weeks holiday. I missed home, the food, the sea, swims in the river, a ride on the horse, freedom to roam over the hills, and my family. Each day was eagerly crossed off on the calendar, until countdown. Bags were packed well before leaving. All girls from the Coast travelled together on the train to Gisborne, then on the service car the next morning for the Coast. Sometimes some of us would take girls from Northland who could not go home for the holidays because of distance and cost. I was always astounded by the comments from the homefolk: 'Gosh, you look so healthy, they must be really feeding you up at school.'

1940s
Granny
~
Lesley Ferguson

Granny is whistling. She always whistles around the house, and I know of no one else's grandmother who whistles the way she does. It's Monday morning, the day Mrs Belcher comes to 'do' for her. Mrs

Belcher is a small brisk woman who lives in one of those narrow old crooked houses close by the Botanical Gardens.

The smell of soapsuds fills the kitchen, and because all the doors are open the smell wafts through from the gas fired copper in the washhouse, across the back porch and the kitchen, eddies around the panelled hall, and out past the heavy jarrah front door. Mrs Belcher blacks the fire grate, cleans the gas cooking range, polishes the tiles, scrubs the steps with hot water and sandsoap, and washes the floors. I hang about on the back porch looking up under the eaves for the four-and-twenty blackbirds that Granny has been whistling about as she pegs the washing on the clothesline.

Cracked concrete slabs pave the backyard path and border a pocket handkerchief sized piece of lawn. Somewhere under the grass and onion weed lies a well, now buried, where according to my mother she and her sister and brother had each to do a hundred pumps every day to get the water up.

The smell of freshly baked fruit buns brings me hopefully inside, where Granny is wrapping some up for Mrs Belcher to take home. Housework completed, it is time to go down to the village. Granny polishes her shoes with the moist inside of banana skins she has saved for the purpose. Her pointed patent leather toes are soon glossy, and as we walk to the shops I watch her feet. They pop in and out beneath her long skirt, pointed, shiny and pointing outwards. It seems to me impossible to walk that way.

Granny is very quick, energetic and lively and loves a good game of tennis. During the 1919 influenza epidemic she and Grandfather were practical and thoughtful, using their new Essex car to help the sick, delivering meals, nursing, minding and cooking.

She is a careful and thorough housekeeper, and when the time comes to sort the attic I don't want to miss out. She sits on the hallstand and directs operations as Monica climbs up the ladder to the attic door. Suitcases and boxes are passed down and they laugh over old clothes.

A black dinner suit appears, 'Alex's dinner suit!'

Gran holds her breath, and I am horrified to see tears start down her face—my stoic Granny. I want to comfort her, and in this moment I learn that I am older, and she is old and vulnerable.

I've wangled an invitation to tea, and it's to be curry, not too hot and sprinkled with soggy sultanas, the way she always does it.

Granny is whistling again, busy in the kitchen, and I set the table for tea.

1950s
First Dance at Tipene
~
Maringi Riddell

Clang! Clang! Clang!

'What's that bell for?' we asked among ourselves as we hurried to the corridor. That was one of the many rules we had to obey at boarding school. If the bell should ring, no matter what time of day, we were to stop what we were doing and get along to the main corridor right away.

Miss Berridge was waiting there, bell in hand, looking rather vexed. When everyone had arrived, she started calling the roll.

'One!'

'Yes, Miss Berridge.'

'Two!'

'Yes, Miss Berridge.'

'Three!'

'Yes, Miss Berridge.'

So it went on until we were all accounted for. My number was fifty-two, and there were eighty-three of us altogether.

'You're too excited, girls—far too excited. If you don't settle down I will call the dance off,' she announced. It was as if a magic wand had been waved over us. We were 'as quiet as' for the rest of the day. Calling off the dance was the last thing we wanted. All week long we had been talking about the forthcoming dance at Tipene, our brother school at Bombay.

As a new girl I'd been told about these wonderful, few and very far between occasions—something to really look forward to, the highlight of the year in fact. The names of several heart-throbs were mentioned again and again: 'Awi Riddell, Ernie Hopa, Tangi Samuels . . . '

My dress was white with green polka dots, one my Auntie Jane had made. It had a long, flared skirt which had to be worn over a full, frilly slip—the fashion at the time. We all went to great pains to make ourselves look as pretty as we could, and we did too, even without makeup, which was another school rule.

The bus ride out to Bombay took forever. And we were so quiet, afraid that even at this late stage the dance might be called off.

As our bus pulled up outside the huge hall, Mr Lewis appeared and greeted us at the door. When we were all inside, the boys, who were lined up on the stage, burst into song—an action song of welcome. The spontaneous, spirited singing quite took my breath away. During the song I found my gaze going back time and again to a strikingly handsome boy. He seemed to have a presence about him—an aura that set him apart.

I asked the girl next to me who he was. She answered, 'That's Awi Riddell, the head prefect.'

(Who was to know then that he would become my husband?)

After the speech of welcome, we all shook hands, and the dance was underway. I thoroughly enjoyed myself that night. I remember that Awi didn't ask me to dance—if we did dance together, it would have been during the Gay Gordons—but there was no shortage of partners.

All too soon it was over. It was time to go. But before getting back onto our bus, we all lined up and shook hands again.

Our bus ride back to Parnell was a noisy one, with everyone chatting happily. Miss Berridge didn't seem to mind. But back at school, before we went upstairs to bed, she announced, 'Girls, there'll be no talking whatsoever from now on. I won't have you disturbing the juniors. Goodnight.'

'Goodnight, Miss Berridge. And thank you,' we chorused. And off to bed we went, still brimming with unspoken words, but quiet as mice.

1940s
Stream of Dreams

~

Heather Williams

They called it Stony Creek although I never saw any stones in it. It flowed through Grandpa's farm, although flow is not really the right word as most of the time it didn't. It was mostly in the winter and after heavy spring and autumn rain that it came alive, and instead of flowing it rushed and tumbled along, leaping over fallen willow logs, snatching at overhanging willow fronds, tugging at the grass growing along its banks, sending searching clawing fingers to dig at the roots, swirling into pools, stirring leaves and sticks into a muddy merry-go-round before continuing on its madly hectic way to join a bigger stream somewhere.

Usually the creek bed was dry and grass-lined with sweetly scented, shy white violets and yellow-eyed daisies growing in shady patches on little grassy knolls. The willows whispered to each other and dipped their trailing green fingers in the cool deep dark pool that remained after the creek had spent itself in wild fury.

It was here I loved to sit and dream, fascinated by the pirouetting fantails as they flicked and twittered catching tiny insects on the wing. Here the white flowered hawthorn raised its thick sheltering arms above the pool and the white petals floated silently down to dimple the smooth black glassy surface.

What deep dark secrets did this pool hold? Was some beautiful golden haired princess held forever captive in its fathomless depths or was it full of wet black slithery slimy slippery eels?

There was another big brown pool further downstream—big and bawdy, flaunting itself in the sunlight. It was always there and never dried up no matter how hot and dry the summer. Here the cows always stopped to drink as they wandered to and from the milking shed, so the edge here was always rough and dusty and, close in, muddy. On opposite sides a bank rose up five or six feet, while the fourth end retreated under the willows, gradually disappearing into a grassy channel.

Here were the eels. Dozens of them! They must have slithered their way here from miles around. With rods cut from the bamboo bush in Nanna's garden, a piece of string gleaned from the pantry string bag, and safety pins as improbable but trusty hooks, two boys from neighbouring farms, my sister and I spent many happy hours eeling, perched somewhat precariously on the bank or on a clump of grass on a ledge part way down the bank. Occasionally the boys would produce a real hook, but once they were lost it was back to safety pins. Amazingly, they worked, so before long we had a dozen or so eels lined up on the bank or slung over the electric fence. Most of them ended up gracing the table of the farmer opposite us.

Robin Hood and his Merry Men versus the Sheriff of Nottingham was another favourite game we played. We usually teamed up with our two friends for this, my sister with Gilmour and me with Bobby.

I liked Bobby because he sometimes let me fly his balsa wood model aeroplanes. I saw myself one day as a pilot. Some of his models used a wound-up rubber band to make the propeller spin, the plane flying quickly through the air before nose-diving to earth. Bobby would quickly retrieve it and anxiously examine it for damage before he'd let me fly it again. Others glided and floated gently on the air.

With bows and arrows fashioned from the trusty bamboo bush we stalked each other among the willows. There was never any Maid

Marion to capture, as the boys couldn't see the point of that, so two by two we were either Robin Hood and Will or the Sheriff of Nottingham and his aide.

Fifty years later I revisited the creek before the farm was sold and passed out of family hands. The willows were still there but some had fallen, and others were bowed with age, pressing closer to the creek bed and concealing more secret pools—places where I now disturbed families of ducks that were never there before to intrude on that place of solitude.

A culvert had been laid across the deep dip that led to the eel pond and it was hard to find the fantail glade, now more deeply concealed than before. As I followed the path of the creek, parting the willow fronds and climbing over fallen logs to find my secret places, I dreamed of bygone days. And, as I heard again those voices from the past, I laid my childhood dreams to rest, there among the willows.

1940s
Where Did It Go?
~
Oho Kaa

There it lay, the most beautiful purse I had ever seen. It had its own handle too. My fingers bumped along the embossed work. On one side there were three pyramids, their sharp peaks silhouetted against the evening sky.

I turned it over and my fingers moved along to an arab sitting on a camel, by a small watering hole. A lady dressed in green and red stood with a tall pitcher on her head. Nearby a little girl was similarly dressed.

My dad had sent me the purse for my seventh birthday, only a few months before he was killed in action. It became the link to the dad I had lost. My name and address were neatly printed inside it. I took it everywhere. Each night it slept under my pillow. I delighted in running my fingers along the different shapes, guessing what they were. I became quite good at this.

It became one of my possessions when I went to St Joseph's. Everyone was excited at June holiday time. My pocket money, my handkerchief, and tickets for the train and bus to take me home were secure in my special purse.

'Ten minutes' refreshments at Wairoa, then we will leave again,' yelled the conductor as he slammed the door behind him. We girls decided to treat ourselves to the refreshments and followed the people out. The canteen was packed. It seemed that everyone was hungry.

'A hot pie and cup of tea please,' I said. I paid and waited. My mates already had their hands full of goodies.

'Come on, we don't want to miss the train,' they urged. I put my purse down on the counter while I reached forward to get my pie and tea. And in that instant it disappeared. My purse! I gasped. My purse had gone. It was nowhere to be seen. Maybe it had dropped on the floor? I looked down, hoping upon hope that it would be there. But no such luck. I looked round desperately.

No one seemed to notice how upset I was. Everyone was minding their own business.

I dragged myself back to the train. No bus ticket to get me home, no money, no purse. I felt so helpless, I cried too. My friends shared their taxi with me to our hotel in Gisborne. Luckily the hotel proprietress was an old girl from St Joseph's and she let me ring home to explain what had happened. Then she spoke to my mother.

'It's okay,' she smiled when she got off the phone.

'I'll see to your ticket for the bus. You can pay me back when you come back from your holiday. Now cheer up.'

She hugged me tight for a long time and when she let me go I felt much better.

I often think of that dreadful day and my special purse—because, up to this day, I wonder, 'Where did it go?'

1930s
The Poultry Parade
~
Shirley Dobbs Signal

Dad has a new job in Motueka and we're living at Stent's Hotel until our house is built. The Stents have a large and robust family, who take me under their collective wing to introduce me to our new town. Today their sons are bringing the hens into the hotel back yard. I scramble up on top of a rickety pile of old boxes. No way am I going to let the Stent boys see I'm scared. Equally, no way am I going to be anywhere near when those hens meet their doom.

One of the boys catches a hen, another raises a chopper. Before my mesmerised gaze it's 'Off with her head,' just like that Queen of Alice's. But the head doesn't come off. It dangles horribly, halfway off, and the hen runs crazily round the yard in ghastly diminishing circles. The others are used to this, they laugh at the fun. I draw my knees right up under my chin. I don't want that dreadful apparition down there anywhere near my feet. It's like taking part in your own horror movie.

One of the Stent sisters, the kind one, looks at my face. It must be ashen. She leans close and whispers, 'It's really dead. Truly. It's just the nerves make it do that.'

I desperately want to believe her . . . but in case she isn't right, I don't want to witness any more botched executions today. When they catch the next hen, I no longer care what the Stent boys think. I shut my eyes tight.

I hope they don't have poultry on the menu tonight.

1940s
Oriental Bay
~
Lesley Ferguson

Although hopeless at arithmetic, I enjoyed the patterns of numerals, so I knew that to be eight on the eighth day of the eighth month was special. All the important people in my world would be with me that day, except for Dad, who was overseas in the army. My mother, brother, granny, Monica, and Aunty (my great aunt) would come for tea. There'd be warmth, fun, cake and presents.

I had handed over my optimistic birthday wish list—pony, silver bangle, leather basketball, and books. Hopeless dreams, I knew, but it felt good to get it off my chest. Intriguing parcels appeared—to be carefully opened so the paper wasn't ruined. There were books from Mother and Monica, and a small shiny torch from Aunty. This would be put to good use, because—best of all—Aunty Betty had invited me to stay the weekend with her.

The birthday tea finished with red jelly in tall glass goblets. The jelly was set just right so that when a spoon was inserted down into it, an interesting jagged cut appeared—and only then could the runny cream be poured in and over it to make a milky opaque pattern. The cream had to be runny. It was passed around the table, each pouring being watched and compared by John and me. Mother made lots of our meals fun.

The torch came in handy when we went out to Aunty's Austin 7. It was a clear cold night—a low moon climbed over the hills as we turned out of Fancourt Street into Hatton Street, then to the main Karori Road where the gleaming tram tracks led us down to town. Then along Lambton Quay to Oriental Bay and into Aunty's narrow angled garage nestled under a rocky bank.

Torchlight led the way up cracking bitumen steps, past a picket fence, along the narrow path bordered with tiny gardens, until I heard the welcome sound of the key in the latch. Everything had a distinctive aged smell: mouldy wood, old dark earth, the tang of salt sea in the air; and then the sound of the gentle lap, lap, slap of the water in the yacht club over the road. It was mysterious in the dark. I couldn't wait to go inside. With the torch we found the light switch. It went on with a ping. It was a tall, narrow old colonial house, one room and staircase wide.

The front living/dining room, filled with family mementos, was again waiting to be explored. It led through to a small kitchen area containing a coal range (unused) and gas stove, dark, with mysterious mouldy earth-backed cupboards. The scullery ran back off this—it was a laundry-cum-kitchen. I stopped to admire again the poster of the Coronation of King George VI, which was fixed to the back door, before making the last call of the night.

Even a trip out to the back room was interesting. Souvenir coronation flags, our New Zealand one and the Union Jack, made of fine silk and mounted on gilt sticks, were hung criss-cross to the wall; and above the bench seat hung a long chain which, when pulled, clank-clanked to flush the round bowl with a frighteningly greedy gurgle.

'Race you upstairs,' called Aunty, sportingly letting me rush up first. The game was to catch the heels of the first one up—not difficult because the stairs were so steep. Thin carpet runner on the stairs was held in place with brass rods, which stopped us from slipping. 'My' room, to the right, was wonderful. Like my aunt's, it had sloping ceilings that followed the roof pitch. Both bedrooms boasted old-fashioned floral pastel wallpapers over scrim, which rustled when the wind blew. A small window looked out to the bank and back yard. The wardrobe was a curtained alcove and behind the curtain were shelves holding an ancient Māori kete, baskets from Niue Island and boxes of old treasures. The little kapok bed on one side of the room invited me into this special space. A basic match-lined bathroom, with gas califont

Wellington Harbour in earlier days, from Aunty Betty's bedroom.

and iron bath, separated the two bedrooms. (Gibbs dental paste for dentures stood on the shelf.)

Gloating, I snuggled into bed, with my new book and torch beside me. Aunty tucked me in. I could see the silver torch in the darkness so, daringly, I turned it on and opened the new *Babar* book . . . Later, 'It's time to sleep, Lesley.' A firm tone and no chuckles. It seemed a good idea to try reading under the covers, and by the time the battery flickered out, my eyes were sore. As I drifted off to sleep the last sound to be heard was a tram rolling along the track, distant at first then clanging past us to fade away towards the Roseneath hill.

Morning bustle woke us. The routine was to go and cuddle into Aunty's bed with her, and play the Lock-Key word game. She was the lock, I was the key, this time.

'I'm a book lock,' she started.

'I'm a book key,' was my reply.

'I'm a torch lock.' (Ooh.)

'I'm a torch key.'

Then the expected: 'I'm a mun lock,' and 'I'm a monkey.'

Giggling hopelessly, we followed up with the rhyme of Adam and Eve and Pinch me . . . Other entertainments followed.

An old brass telescope stood in the corner by Aunty's bedroom window. She opened the window wide, screwed up one eye, and peered through the 'scope to focus on the launches and dinghies opposite. Then it was my turn. The boats jumped at me, busily coming and going past the sea wall. I was fascinated at the sights, sounds and smells which drifted up to our second storey viewpoint.

When we'd spied out to sea long enough, Aunty took me out to the yard, where a steep rotten rock cliff loomed up behind the back of the house. Morning glory scrambled up the rocks, tangling over some rickety steps that led to a lookout. Halfway up, higher than the house roof, was a platform, and above that was an arch of whalebone by a bench seat. All very precarious, but the view was a prize.

The following year, September 1942, the Royal Port Nicholson Yacht Club agreed to lease the area to the American navy for the duration of the war. Temporary buildings were erected, cutting out my aunt's view, and a naval repair depot for landing craft was established. The Yacht Club became a hospital for malaria victims, until November 1944. The temporary buildings later became a boys' hostel.

1930s
Christmas
~
Heather Williams

'Wake up! Wake up! Quick! It's Christmas morning. Has Santa been? What has he left for us?' Sure enough, there were the balloons at the foot of our beds. He must have been.

With bated breath, eyes agleam and shrieking with delight, we turned our stockings upside-down to shake out all sorts of small toys, bubble pipes, mouth organs, new socks, coloured pencils, and there, there at the very bottom, AN ORANGE. One whole round gleaming orange, and nuts! Nuts to crack. Nuts to savour. Which to eat first? Or should we keep them a little longer, just to look at and hold and treasure?

Daddy always believed in having them, so tooting whistles and banging drums were also part of Christmas.

The church bells always rang out more joyfully on Christmas morning. We sang those lovely carols about the baby Jesus and the angels, shepherds and kings. Somehow people seemed to greet each other more cheerfully.

The next exciting part was the journey to our grandparents' farm in Daddy's pride and joy, our little brown fabric-covered baby Austin. On arrival, we'd be hugged and kissed, our curly heads patted, and we'd run into the big front hall. There on the enormous chair under the cuckoo clock one year were the two most beautiful dolls you ever did see—just waiting to be picked up and cuddled, as we were.

Christmas dinner was a wonderful occasion: the huge dining room table all set with silver and crystal on a snow-white cloth, and candles and bon bons (to be opened later), wondrous crackers that held paper hats, jokes and lovely necklaces of little glass beads or silver trinkets for bracelets. Sometimes I was allowed to decorate the table with a vase of geraniums and white daisies.

The French doors opened into the conservatory and the perfume of the hoya drifted through the room. We all sat around, grandparents, uncles, aunts, Mother and Daddy, my sister and I. With heads bowed, grace was said and thanks given for God's good provision and blessings on each one of us.

Grandpa always carved the turkey, a portion on each plate. The best bone china dinner set was brought out for the occasion. We served ourselves from steaming dishes of vegetables, among which were the first new potatoes and peas of the season, freshly gathered from Grandpa's garden and smelling of mint.

Later Nanna brought in the steaming hot plum pudding, topped with holly and all ablaze with brandy fire, holding it high for all to see. Concealed in that blue-flamed delight (and eagerly sought by each of us) were small coins and sterling silver trinkets.

Afterwards the men sat and enjoyed cigars and brandy. I love the smell of cigars to this day. They conjure up such memories of childhood Christmases long ago. The ladies retired to the kitchen to deal with the enormous stack of dishes, without the benefit of a dishwasher! My sister and I went outside to play. I was so glad to be a child.

The cows were brought in early on Christmas Day so we could attend the evening service at the little church in the village where my uncles tolled the bell. I loved that time, all warm and happy, squeezed between my grandparents and parents in the family pew—but it was so hard to stay awake.

1930s
Mr Hudson and the Glow-worm
~
Joyce Harrison

It may well have begun with the bloodsucker sting, that surprising mess of squashed red wings and legs; but I liked to think of my fascination with insects as starting on the day when, coming home from school, I found on the track that huge triangle of green-grey moth right at my feet. It seemed like a gift dropped specially for me from heaven. The moth did not fly away at my touch for it was quite dead, its wings spread like pieces of velvet astride its furry body. They covered the palm of my hand as I carefully bore my treasure home.

Dad made me a display case from a cigarette tin lined with scarlet felt. In due course the moth had for company a black beetle, a white butterfly and a ladybird. Proper scientific names were called for, especially in the case of the most prized exhibit, the green moth. Again Dad came up with the answer: who better to be consulted than Mr Hudson, the famous naturalist, who lived in an old verandahed house less than a block away?

A visit, it appeared, would be well received. Dad was the escort; I carried the cigarette tin. The panelled door was opened by a white-haired gnome, bent over no doubt by too many years of peering at butterfly wings. He led the way into a dim room, quiet as a museum, the walls lined with giant chests of narrow drawers.

Mr Hudson admired the contents of the tin, awarding a name to each specimen. (Fancy New Zealand insects having their own names in Latin, all ready, waiting to be claimed!) Then he turned to his own collection. In and out slid the drawers: row upon row of moths in one, another a mosaic of patterned butterflies. These were followed by first beetles and then dragonflies, each a shade different from the rest, and each spiked with a long slender pin.

The cigarette tin had clearly been upstaged. I persuaded Dad to hunt out a large cylindrical milk powder tin with a press-in lid. He fashioned four squares of pinex, sawing off the corners, so that they would slip easily through the round opening of the tin. Through the centre of each he bored a hole to take a dowelling rod. The pieces were then spaced on the rod to resemble a tiered cake plate. But what cakes! First a cockroach, then a katydid, and then, daringly, a weta and a large woolly spider.

Childhood

I had to steel myself to learn from Dad the process of etherising and then slitting open and cleaning out my specimens before stuffing them with cottonwool. The weta and the spider made me squeamish before I even touched them. (A worry indeed for someone planning to make a career of it . . .)

From time to time I proudly took my collection down to Mr Hudson. He kindly printed the strange names on cards to go with each item, straight from his amazing memory. I secretly hoped that I would one day bring him a specimen never seen before. I pictured him suddenly jolting forward, his white eyebrows raised, staring through the bottom of his glasses, reaching for his magnifying glass. 'Could this be a . . . no . . . I believe you've come up with a totally new species!' It never happened, of course; but Mr Hudson seemed to enjoy our little sessions, and willingly brought out yet more drawers of gauzy wings and spindly legs, even after I had run out of brand-new things to say about them.

It was a little sad all the same, I reflected one day, to think of all those butterflies fluttering among the flowers in the sunshine and then being stretched out stiff and still, stuck with sharp pins and packed away for ever in tier upon tier of stifling graves. I glanced round the room. The grey photos on the dark panelling began to close in on me. I looked quickly away . . .

'When I grow up,' I said, as to a colleague, 'I'm going to be a naturalist.'

'Oh no you won't,' said Mr Hudson, as to a nine-year-old child.

By now I felt familiar enough to argue with the great man. 'Yes I will.'

'We'll see,' said Mr Hudson, and we left it at that.

Better than collecting and killing the insects, however, was keeping them as pets. While my schoolmates saw little charm in my stuffed bugs, they found unexpected entertainment in live katydids, brought to school in a netting-fronted cage. Set in the sun on the windowsill during an arithmetic test, they began to rasp out their 'Pst! Pst!' with nicely spaced pauses between, providing a hilarious diversion for the class.

At fourteen I was allowed to go exploring after dark in the neighbouring bush reserve where I found a bank of glow-worms. I managed to manoeuvre one onto the end of a stick and carry it home. I set it among the ferns in the garden where it continued its hopeful shining. But how to preserve this tiny creature that was scarcely more than a beam of light? You couldn't stuff it, cage it, or even feed it . . . Then I had an inspiration—why not a poem?

TO A GLOW-WORM

That some small foolish winged thing I might be
To fly unfearing to this starry cave,
These shining halls and blue-lit balconies,
And all the foils of thy weird cruelty, brave.

That innocent in joy I might approach
Thy curtain hung with jewels twinkling bright;
And in thy web slow twining round my wings,
Forget the gloomy shadows of this night.

Next time I passed the old house I paused. Mr Hudson, I knew, was gone; not, I supposed, to be impaled on one of his pins, but to some amorphous heaven above and beyond the ancient macrocarpa which still overhung his lawn.

'You were right, Mr Hudson,' I called to his shade. 'I'm not going to be a naturalist after all. I'm going to be a poet.'

1930s
Friendship

~

Rachelle Calkoen

The year was 1933, and Chel was just nine years old. A happy, carefree, outgoing child, she loved everything and everybody. She adored her sisters, her home, her school. As one of those children who could find enjoyment in almost everything she sometimes made it difficult for her parents to find a punishment for her that she wouldn't turn into some sort of game. Nothing had ever darkened her horizon until the day Sara came up to her in class.

'Chel, would you come to my house this afternoon?' Sara asked. 'Mary is coming too.'

'That would be great,' said Chel, and the three of them set out together on the long walk to Sara's house. Mary and Sara were whispering together, but Chel didn't take any notice—she was skipping contentedly along, expectant that they would probably tell her later what it was all about.

When they came to the corner of Sara's street, Mary and Sara suddenly started running as fast as they could. Chel was taken by surprise, and consequently ran a short distance behind them. As soon as they reached Sara's house they slammed the door shut. Chel could hear the two of them laughing behind the door, and heard their feet climbing the stairs to the first floor, where Sara's parents lived. Puzzled, she stood in front of the door thinking they were playing a game. She heard a window opening and looked up to see Mary and Sara's laughing faces looking down on her.

'Stay there!' Sara called out. 'I'm just going to brush my teeth.' This seemed a rather strange remark. The two girls disappeared, but not for long. They came back to the window with a toothbrush full of toothpaste and a beaker of water. Sara brushed her teeth until her whole mouth foamed. Then she took a mouthful of water and spat it out on to Chel's upturned face.

'Take that, you dirty Jew,' she called, laughing loudly as they shut the window.

Chel slowly walked away. Her auntie lived just around the corner, and that is where she went.

'Come in Chel!' Auntie Annie sounded pleased to see her. 'We haven't had a visit from you for a long time. But child, what's the matter, I've never seen you look so miserable. What is it?' With that Chel burst into tears and, faltering and stammering between big sobs, she described what had happened.

Auntie washed her face gently, made a cup of hot Milo, and took her home. It was good to be in a loving environment again, but the pain of betrayal stayed for years.

1950s
UE English
~
Maringi Riddell

Mrs Barry, my English teacher, was a memorable person—large, likeable and passionate about her subject. She made Shakespeare come alive for us; taught us how to analyse poems; improved our grammar considerably; and was kind enough to invite our Sixth Form English class to her home to lunch one Sunday afternoon, a real treat for boarding school students.

She'd brought us all through School Certificate English, and here we were, a few days away from our University Entrance English examination. Her last-minute advice was clear: 'Read the instructions at least three times through, and spend at least ten minutes selecting questions and planning your answers.'

Monday morning, the day of our exam, dawned clear and fine. Because our school was so small, we had to sit our exam at Auckland University, a good half-hour's walk away. So we set off with plenty of time to spare. As we walked we chattered cheerfully, happy to be free of the confines and restraints of school. It was quite unsettling, to arrive at the university not knowing where to go, and with hundreds of other students already there. However, it wasn't long before we were all seated and ready to go.

By this time I was feeling really nervous, and when I'm nervous my hands perspire. I had to mop up before I could hold my pen properly.

'You may start now!' the supervisor announced, after a long spiel of instructions. I turned my paper over and glanced quickly at the instructions. My heart sank. What a lot to do in three hours! I collected my jumbled thoughts, took a deep breath and ripped into it. My pen flew across the lines, filling page after page. As the minutes ticked quickly by I was vaguely aware of the supervisor crossing off each fifteen-minute span. There was no way I was going to finish on time. My hand ached with the effort of writing so frantically.

'Would you please put down your pens,' came the dreaded command. I gasped with disappointment. I still had a couple more questions to answer. How on earth did they expect anyone to get all that done in three hours? I put down my pen and closed up my answer booklet. As I turned back to the cover page, the instructions hit me in the eye. Right at the top of the page, in bold print, it said: ANSWER NO MORE THAN SIX QUESTIONS.

I couldn't believe it. I hadn't seen it. I'd tried to answer them all. No wonder I didn't have enough time. A big lump formed in my throat. My eyes filled with tears. I knew I had blown it. After all my hard work, I'd blown it. My brain went numb. There was nothing I could do but hand in my paper and go.

By the time I got back to school I'd cried myself dry. Mrs Barry was waiting for us. She took one look at me and asked, 'Have you been crying?' That set me off again. I blurted out my stupid mistake and waited for her to scold me. Instead, she gave me a big hug and said, 'No postmortems. Forget all about it now and prepare for the next one.'

I knew she was right, but it was helluva hard to put that out of my mind.

All summer holiday I worried about my results. We'd been told that we'd receive them in mid-January, but because I lived in the wop-wops, I'd have to wait a couple of days or so extra.

Auntie Daph rang me up on one of those long, hot days, saying that the University Entrance results were in the *Dominion*. She finished off by saying, 'I can't find your name.'

I gasped, feeling my heart lurch, 'Are you sure?'

'I'm sure,' she answered. I felt sick in my stomach. I just couldn't bring myself to tell the rest of the family, so I quietly slipped out of the house and went around to Auntie Daph's to see for myself. She was one of the few people in our extended family who bought an outside paper.

Her home was three miles away, down Kaitara Lane, and there was no other way to get there but by shank's pony. What a relief it was to find that it was the University Scholarship results that were printed out, and not the Entrance results. My auntie didn't know the difference. I gave her a big hug, telling her that I was thrilled by her mistake. I had another life yet.

Two days later I received my envelope. The rural delivery man had been and gone, and I hadn't even noticed. There the envelope lay in the mailbox—long, brown, and windowed. It took an eternity to rip it open and unfold the paper. I gasped in astonishment. I'd passed with a comfortable margin. Screaming with joy I rushed back to the house. Life was great!

1940s
Away from Home
~
Heather Williams

The day had inevitably arrived. Reluctantly, my sister and I were on our way to boarding school, dressed in the uniform of the Wanganui Girls' College: navy serge costumes, long-sleeved white blouses, school tie, long black woollen stockings, black lace-up shoes, navy velour hat complete with band and school crest, gloves and a small navy handbag.

Our trunks carried the usual items of clothing including a navy serge gym frock with three box pleats back and front and tied with a navy girdle; black Italian cloth bloomers; a black velvet, lace-trimmed frock for Saturday evening wear, and a long-sleeved cream tussore silk frock to wear to church in the summer.

Mother made all these garments, her feet rhythmically pedalling a treadle sewing machine while reels of thread flew through the needle. Our job was to make, by hand, the dozens of buttonholes, sew on buttons, and label each garment with a 'Cashew' name tag.

With lumps in our throats and hearts in our boots we kissed our mother and uncles goodbye, and humped our trunks to our respective dormitories, where we proceeded to unpack. Later, the matron, Miss Aldridge, would inspect our drawers to see if our possessions were tidy and clearly marked with our names. A prefect or senior girl showed us around the school buildings, the dining room, the common room where we assembled for prayers every night after prep, the locker room with its pigeonholes for shoes and cleaning gear, the assembly hall, swimming pool, tennis court and classrooms.

The worst part of boarding school was the cold shower or bath every girl was on her honour to take every morning, winter and summer. Hot baths were a twice-a-week luxury. Saturday mornings after breakfast it was to the common room, where Miss Aldridge would inspect freshly polished shoes, neatly darned socks or stockings, cleaned and pressed uniforms, and replaced missing buttons. Darning required the hole to be filled with a neat pattern of woven wool—any edges cobbled together would be cut out by Miss Aldridge, thus leaving an even bigger hole to be mended.

Saturday afternoons, if it wasn't an 'outing Saturday', all the boarders were assembled for the customary two-hour walk in 'crocodile file'—two by two, in the charge of the resident teachers. Our reward, when we returned, was a luxury cream bun. Saturday night was 'pay night' when each girl received a shilling to be spent like this: sixpence for two threepenny stamps, threepence for the plate in church, and threepence for three pieces of barley sugar.

Because of the series of strong earthquakes during 1942, earthquake drill was practised twice a week before breakfast. We each had to go to the nearest exit—usually a window on to a fire escape—climb down the ladder which finished several feet up, and jump to the ground. We also had to learn how to carry each other in a fireman's grip in case the need arose.

Our contribution to the war effort was making camouflage nets. These were set up in the common room. We were expected to spend any spare moment we had throwing the coarse hemp-threaded shuttle to form knots in the four to six inch mesh. When one net was finished another was set up.

The headmistress, Miss Baker, always took prayers on Sunday night. The busy click click of her high-heeled shoes announced her imminent arrival. Silence would descend upon the girls and in she'd sweep, wearing a pretty, soft flowing evening gown similar to those the Queen Mother currently wears. Her immaculately groomed curly grey hair framed a round face with piercing blue eyes that missed nothing. Shoulders back, and head held high, she seemed taller than she was.

The boarders' picnic was a highlight of the first term. We all piled aboard the old paddle steamer for the trip up river to the deserted settlement at Pipiriki for the day.

Before the war, staff were employed to prepare meals, set the tables and wash dishes. Boarders were now rostered for these duties. Part of one of the rhymes the older girls used to say was:

> No more maids dressed in black
> Pouring gravy down our backs

In winter the prefect at the head of the table had to see that each girl took her teaspoonful of what we called 'Mickey's Morning Muck'—a horrid tasting emulsion which was supposed to keep us well.

Time passed, and with the return of my father from overseas, boarding school days drew to an end. In some ways I was sorry, but in others I was pleased to be going home. Besides, I had yet to meet my new baby brother, now three months old.

1930s
Three Penn'orth of Dog's Meat
~
Joyce Harrison

On my weekly visit to the butcher's shop I was always prepared to give my order, but Mrs Bowser would glance down at me across the counter and get in first: 'Three penn'orth of dog's meat.' From the serious way in which she said it, I could have been wanting ten pounds' worth of their best steak. Not that Chummie wasn't important. He was my own special dog, and it was my job each Friday to go and collect his parcel of bones.

I enjoyed the challenge of manoeuvring to be served by Mrs Bowser rather than by her husband or the apprentice, knowing that she would work really hard to get Chummie a good deal. She would set off round the shop, picking over scraps on the great wooden chopping block, rummaging in the scrap bin, plonking her finds on my square of newsprint each time she passed the counter. I'd will her to go out to the back, and usually, sooner or later, she would oblige and return with a special tidbit. Perhaps even a sheep's tongue, holding it up for my inspection before adding it to the grisly pyramid.

'How's that?' her look would ask, and I would nod and beam my approval. If she was in the mood she would then pick up the great knife and slash off a loose piece from one of the carcasses hanging along the wall. I watched a little nervously when she passed by her husband in case she absentmindedly sliced a sliver off the back of his neck. He was so fat, he mightn't even have missed it!

Mr and Mrs Bowser were both large people, all over. I reckoned this was probably because they ate so much of their juicy red meat. I could picture her serving up their Sunday roast and, looking at her husband's rosy face, saying: 'Just one more slice, dear . . . and another little bit . . .'

If Mr Bowser happened to notice my meat mountain, he would screw up his lips and raise his eyebrows. Long since, I decided that this was just a formality. When the parcel was at last being wrapped I would think of Chummie, stretched out on the back lawn, one floppy ear spread along the grass, eye half closed, adjusting his jaw around a huge knuckle bone and curling his wet tongue round its silvery sheen . . .

It would be hard to explain why Mrs Bowser was such a favourite with me, because it wasn't just for the meat. She could surely never have been called beautiful and nowadays her very white face, big white teeth and very black hair, squeezed under a black hairnet to keep it away from the meat, made me wonder if she was what my mother meant by 'having a face like the back of a bus'. Our understanding was certainly not based on looks, any more than it needed words.

One day my friend Minnie came in with me to the Bowsers on our way home, she having been unable to persuade me to buy us three penn'orth of fish'n'chips instead. Her eyes grew bigger as my pile of goodies rose. When we had eased our way out of the spring door she couldn't wait to declare her outrage. 'You're lucky! You get more for threepence than we do for our six penn'orth of cat's meat. Do you think they reckon that cats have got smaller mouths?'

Childhood

'I didn't know you had a cat,' I said. 'What's it like?'

'We haven't,' responded Minnie, 'But Mum makes gorgeous soup.'

I was shocked. Did Mrs Bowser believe in Minnie's cat? Minnie wouldn't bother to be too convincing. She didn't bother much about facts generally. Even her name was made up. It was supposed to be Mimosa. What else might she get away with? What if Mrs Bowser had guessed Minnie's secret and thought that my mother was also just making soup? We did need to be careful with money because of the Depression, but we hadn't come down to conning the butcher into feeding us on the cheap. However, the more I thought on it, the more suspect my visits to the Bowsers began to appear. For one thing, we did not buy our own meat there, and I could hardly explain that we

Joyce, aged 8, with companion Chummie.

patronised the butcher with the van to save my mother from carrying one more heavy parcel up our steep hill.

On Wednesday mornings Chummie would be first to hear the engine away down the hill by the beach, and if he was in the kitchen he would go frantic to be let loose. Out through the gate he would race, ready to dance round the driver's door as the van slowed. The butcher would chat for a while, partly to keep him guessing but mostly because Chummie was his favourite dog. Then he would swing open his back doors and present his special friend with a free bone. It wouldn't be tactful to tell Mrs Bowser about that either, although on the other hand it might convince her that we really did own a pet.

If it weren't for the notice in the shop saying NO DOGS ALLOWED I could perhaps take him down and show her. I could even hold him up to the shop window. Best of all, though, would be if I told her the story of how I came to get him. She might be satisfied.

The following Friday it was Mr Bowser who came over to take my order. I kept my head firmly down, studying the chart beside the till with a picture of a cow and all the different shapes into which it could be cut. After all, the poster was meant to be looked at, or why hang it up? Not that it made much sense. When Mrs Bowser's customer went out I lost interest in rumps and blades and moved over quickly to catch her attention. My story tumbled out before Mrs Bowser could say a word:

'Our dog's a cocker spaniel,' I informed her. 'Shiny black with a white chest and one white paw. I wanted him from when I was four but I had to wait until I was eight and old enough to look after him. He came on my birthday last year. I went home for lunch specially and there was a scrabbling noise under the kitchen table, and out came this wee black puppy, squirming, but all bent round like a horseshoe. I had to shout to Mum, "What's the matter with him?" She said it was just that he liked me and wanted to be friends. Then he horseshoed round the other way so I knew he was all right. I picked him up all warm and wriggly and he licked my nose . . . '

Mrs Bowser was standing quite still watching me, as was Mr Bowser and the apprentice. So were a couple of customers who had come in. She had a funny smile on just one side of her mouth, without showing any of her teeth, and then she said, 'He must be a great companion.'

She thought of that word. She chose it, so she must now believe for sure that Chummie was real. That meant that life and dog's meat could go on as before. As Dad would say, 'Business as usual.'

CHILDHOOD

1920s
Holidays in the Vosges
~
Jeannette Hunter

It was August when the big girls had their summer holidays—it was a special time that the whole family enjoyed together. Every summer we went somewhere for the vacation, sometimes in Holland but often in Belgium, France or Switzerland. This year it was going to be in the Vosges, in north-east France.

My parents had booked a hotel for three weeks, the train tickets were in Father's pocket, suitcases were packed, people engaged to look after the house, garden and puss, and here was I putting a spoke in the wheel!

'Oh no! Oh, what a nuisance,' worried my mother, peering at me when she came to wake me up, the day before we were due to leave. 'What are we going to do now?'

'Jo, come and have a look,' she called to my father.

I hadn't been well for a few days, not at all my usual laughing self. Now it was obvious why I hadn't been happy—I had the measles!

'What are we going to do?' asked my mother again—they could not take a sick six-year-old on a train journey that would take nearly the whole day . . .

'We can't cancel the bookings now,' said my father, 'and the other girls will be very disappointed if we're not going.'

A few telephone calls later, and the problem was solved. Mother bundled me in several blankets and took me by taxi—we didn't have a car—with my suitcase, to her parents. I felt very sorry for myself, lying there on a couch in the dark, stuffy study of my unmarried aunt, imagining how my sisters skipped in green flower fields, or splashed through little streams in the sun.

My grandmother, Anja, tried to cheer me up with little presents, Grandfather read stories or drew nice pictures on a blackboard, and Aunt Stel played cards or boardgames with me. Mina, their rotund cook, wobbled into the room with my favourite dishes. I started to enjoy being thoroughly spoiled!

There was good news two days later when my father's sisters visited me. Aunt Jeannette, the paediatrician, examined me and pronounced the liberating words: 'She hasn't got measles, you know. It must have been a sort of heat rash. If her temperature stays normal she can go the day after tomorrow.' Then Aunt Phien told me that as soon as I was better we would go together by train to spend the rest of the holidays with the family. So I missed very little of our three weeks in the mountains after all.

They were happy days, as were all our holidays—and as are all the memories of those times. Oh, the huge brown lollipops my sisters discovered in the village shop! They tasted of licorice, were hard and lasted so long they made our mouths quite sore, but there have never been better tasting ones.

On the way back from one of our long walks in the mountains behind the hotel my father found, as usual, a little 'short cut'. This had happened so often before that we called it, in Dutchified French, Father's 'raccourcietje'—his short cuts always ended up being much longer than the original track. On this occasion the path ended in an alpine meadow from where we had to find our way as best we could, scrambling down the steep side of a mountain.

I have never been a mountaineering hero, being prone to vertigo, so I flatly refused to go one more step, no matter how much the family encouraged or threatened me. In the end, Father—overriding Mother's anxiety—said, 'All right, we are going, you can stay here if you want to,'—and off they went: Father in front, then Dora and Clara, then our nanny with four-year-old Chel on her shoulders, and last my mother calling me to come, please. I shook my head, stubbornly. There I stood in a silent world, the voices of my family quickly fading with only the tick, tick, tick of small stones dislodging from the slopes above me, bounding and slipping on their way to the valley below.

'Would there be wolves in a spot like this . . . or even bears?' I wondered. I quickly set off in the direction I had seen the others disappearing. Far below I could just see the red windjacket of Chel going into the trees. I don't think I ever got down a mountain so fast.

I could see the family not far ahead when I emerged from the copse, but I was aware of my father walking behind me. How did he get there? In front of me was a weird, frightening landscape—a forest of white and grey crosses as far as the eye could see, in straight lines on both sides of the path, sideways, in front, and in long diagonal lines. I didn't know anything about the Great War, but this cemetery of French and German soldiers gave me a tremendous shock. It was the saddest thing I have ever seen.

1950s
Milking
~
Maringi Riddell

During the school holidays, Awi and I took our grandchildren, Mahaki and Ramari, to Rotorua for a few days. While we were there we took them to see the agricultural show at the Agrodome.

During the show the compere asks for volunteers among the children to come up and milk the cow. Mahaki jumped up immediately and was the first one onto the stage. He was really excited. After a couple of fairly successful squirts, he retired to let the other children have a go. Six children later—two squirts each—yielded about a tablespoon of milk, just enough for a cuppa. And at the end of the 'performance' each child was given a Certificate of Udderance. What a laugh! It made me think back to my milking experiences.

I'd been brought up with cows and I must have been about eight years old when I learnt to milk them. My dad had a small dairy farm, and he and Mum milked about forty cows. When Dad went off to war, our cows were transferred over to the much bigger adjoining whānau farm, and Mum helped out often with the milking. Of course Kelly and I had to go with her to the shed. We loved to help out with the separating. We'd get the handle whirring away, then in a little while the cream would begin to pour out of one spout and the milk out of the other.

Towards the end of the war my dad was killed in Italy, and the situation at home changed. Our cows were absorbed permanently into the main herd and Mum, Kelly and I went to live with Nanny Waioeka at Mafeking, three miles away. Here we had a house cow. It was a Jersey, and had been carefully chosen from the main herd by my uncle. We called her Creamy, and she was a wonderful pet. She was the nearest thing we had to a horse, and she was quite happy for us to ride her. Even though we were poor, Creamy had a canvas cover to wear during winter.

We usually milked her in a single wooden cowbail—much less trouble than milking her out in the paddock. We soon found out what a nuisance it was to have to follow her around with the bucket as she sought out juicy clumps of grass to munch on.

During summer it was a pleasant task to milk Creamy, and we all took turns to do it. However, in the winter, on cold, wet days, it wasn't at all pleasant. But the job had to be done. No matter what, she had to be milked, morning and night.

On frosty mornings, before breakfast, I'd go and look for her, and usually find her lying in a sheltered place chewing her cud, and definitely not in the mood to be milked. I had to do all sorts of things to get her to her feet. The most effective thing was to grab hold of her tail and twist it upwards. She hated that, and I hated doing it, but she wouldn't budge otherwise. To keep warm I'd walk along hard up against her, taking care not to let her tramp on my feet.

Once in the bail, I'd tie up her back leg (the one nearest to me) and then wash her teats. Sitting on the milking stool with the bucket angled between my legs, and held firmly between my knees and ankles, I'd start milking. I'd get into the rhythm of pulling down on the teats, right front and back left and, when those two were empty, left front and right back. The music of the milk squirting into the empty bucket would start out as a high-pitched sound, then gradually the notes would come down the scale as the bucket filled. With my head against her rump I couldn't help but feel a strong sense of togetherness.

Most of the time Creamy would happily part with her milk and I'd get three-quarters of a bucket. But on a bad day, when she was feeling mean, she'd hold onto her milk and I'd be lucky to get a quarter of a bucket, and there was nothing I could do about it either.

Flies and sandflies were a real pain at times because she would either flick her tail, whipping me in the face, or kick, to get rid of them. And if you weren't quick enough, over the bucket would go. In order to stop this happening, one of us would have a switch of mānuka to wave around and keep her free of flies.

Milking done, I'd strain the milk into a wide basin and put it into the safe to set. (It wasn't until I was ten that Mum bought our first fridge.) In the morning we'd skim off the cream with a special cream skimmer. This thick double cream was just superb on porridge, desserts, or with fresh bread and jam—a real country treat—something I haven't had since.

A very sad thing about having cows in those days was that they were susceptible to getting 'the bloat'. Creamy suffered with this, and despite calling in the vet at an early stage, she died. It was awful! We cried and cried, and I can still remember her being towed away by the tractor, her belly all swollen, and her head lolling from side to side. A day or so later we had another handpicked cow to replace her, and we called her

Creamy too. It wasn't long before she became one of the family as well. This bloating business happened fairly often, and we went through several Creamies. Many years later we heard that one of the most effective ways to save a cow suffering with bloat was to stab it directly in the stomach to release the built-up air. I certainly wouldn't have been able to handle that.

As we grew to be teenagers, milking cows became a real pest of a job. If there was a powercut (and they happened often) my uncle would come down and collect us all to go up to the whānau farm to milk the herd by hand. It was a difficult job as we were used to milking only one cow. Our hands would ache with the strain of milking several cows on end. Christmas Eve was another time when we were expected to go and help out with the milking, so that it was done quickly and we'd all be able to go into Gisborne to enjoy the night's festivities.

When I went off to Queen Vic at the age of sixteen, I'd had enough of milking. I vowed I would never milk another cow. To this day I've kept my vow, but I think that in those earlier years I more than earned my Certificate of Udderance—don't you?

1940s
Too (Two?) Shy

~

Shirley Dobbs Signal

It's time for the end-of-year Standard Six Dance. Our association with the Island Bay Primary School is shortly coming to an end.

Adelaide comes to me, giggling: 'Tom says would you come to the dance with him?'

I've had very little to do with Tom. He's a nice looking, clever but quiet boy, but I know practically nothing about him. I can't help blushing, and say shyly to Adelaide, 'Tell Tom "Yes, thank you"'.

Adelaide giggles again, and goes back across the room. Our class starts up straight away, but I have time to think—and have my doubts. I don't quite know where I am. Adelaide is such a practical joker. Has Tom really invited me to the dance with him? Or has she just made it all up? After all, I can't just go and ask him, because then he'll feel as if he has to ask me anyway.

The next two weeks are very unsettling. For this event the girls will be wearing the twelve-year-old equivalent of ball gowns; this is always a 'swept-up' affair. I was a bridesmaid a few months ago, so I'll wear my bridesmaid's dress. It's forget-me-not blue, with little pale cream roses here and there. I think I look quite nice in it, but—horror and uncertainty—will I be all dressed up and waiting, and then find that no one turns up to escort me?

The night at last. Mother has curled my hair with the curling tongs, testing the tongs with newspaper first so as not to singe my hair. My father has the car ready to drive us down to Saint Hilda's Hall. I'm standing in the kitchen, waiting. They tell me I look lovely. The doorbell rings and I'm sent off to open the door. I do, shyly. He stands there, just as shy, and looking positively shined up for the evening.

It wasn't one of Adelaide's jokes after all. He really has asked me to the dance.

1950s
Shell Shock
~
Lesley Ferguson

As a family we are great consumers of books, and now that the May holidays have arrived I can forget study and indulge in our favourite form of escapism. Soon I am absorbed in the latest book.

The sun is pouring through the window onto my neck. With racing heart I follow Beau Geste as he creeps around the fortifications. Across the heat-seared desert he tries to locate the approaching marauders. His fellow legionnaires are apparently dead, wounded or useless. Desperately he loads each dead man's rifle, and running at a crouch fires each rifle in turn, hoping to confuse the enemy. My eyes are glued to the page, my hands are sweating with excitement.

There is a click, a soft footfall. The scalp at the back of my head crawls, I daren't breathe, my hands are rigid. This is too real; this is here, not in some foreign desert . . . Another step on the carpet; only my eyes are able to move, taking in a man, his back towards me. He reaches out towards the Chinese lion on the mantelpiece, taking the cigarette from between its gilded teeth and starting to turn towards me.

In a silent rush I am at the sunporch doorway, a cushion clutched as a weapon.

'What are you doing here? Who are you?' My voice is not normal.

Startled, he turns, and I register his eyes, clear blue, wide, and shocked.

'The cigarette? Oh, I was looking for the Millers' house.' He is English, well spoken, smart looking.

'How did you get in?'

'I came in the back door, it was open.'

Ah! That click sound that I'd hardly registered hadn't been part of the story . . . now, get him out, hurry . . .

'This way! I'll show you where the Millers are.' I stride past, foolishly turning my back to him, as I hurry down the passage and out the back door. At the gate I point out the Millers' drive.

'I'm sorry I frightened you,' he apologises.

Shaking legs take me back inside. I lock the doors not knowing whether to scream or cry. I do know I want my mother. I go first to the broom cupboard, take down the Boer War gun, conscious of its heaviness, coldness and oiliness. Then I phone Mum at work.

'Mum, I'm holding the Boer War gun, and I'm scared.' I don't want to hear her impersonal secretary voice; I need the comfort of her Mother voice.

'There was a man in the house . . . and . . . ' the story tumbles out.

'Please put the gun away, I'll be home at once.' Cool, calm, distanced.

Later Mother phones Mrs Miller who comes over to see us and apologises to me for the fright I have had.

'He has been visiting my daughter recently, but has been asked not to come again. He is a war victim, wounded and mentally disturbed, it seems,' she explains sadly.

In spite of my shock I feel sad for the Miller girl and the handsome young man. My busy imagination runs around the results of the recent war, my father's war—P. C. Wren's exciting story of Beau Geste's desert battle lies forgotten for the rest of the day.

1940s
My Aunt Selma

~

Mavis Boyd

We lived on a farm, but in the town four miles away lived my father's sister. Widowed at quite an early age and with no children, she was a tall, dignified, attractive woman with lovely blue-grey eyes, a pink complexion and a nice smile. She used to sew clothes for us, attend our birthdays and Christmas celebrations and would sometimes have us to stay. This must have been quite challenging for her. She had a beautiful house, which she kept in immaculate order, while we were brought up in a much more casual fashion.

I loved going to stay with her. I relished the meals. It was not that they were better than we had at home, where food was always abundant. But they were different and, as with everything else, there was a sense of order and decorum, the maintenance of a certain standard. And there were always little treats which we did not get at home.

Aunt Selma was probably quite gifted artistically. As a young woman she painted in oils and evidence of her work hung all around her attractive house. She sang in a choir, played the piano and church organ, was an excellent seamstress, and made curtains for a drapery shop whenever they had orders. She could make enchanting posies of flowers to give for birthdays or special occasions.

Here was a woman accomplished in domestic and home-making skills, a good conversationalist and a good hostess, as were many other women of her generation. What distinguished her and made her so special was that she exhibited to a remarkable degree the gift of enjoyment. She enjoyed all kinds of things. It could be something very simple, like a piece of hot buttered toast; or a dress that she had made of some especially nice material. She loved the sight of large gum trees with their green-grey foliage, towards the end of summer when the grass under them has been bleached to a golden straw colour. It was something about the colour contrast that stirred her enthusiasm. She also delighted in the spring countryside, when the grass was fresh and green and we went on our annual picnics into the nearby hills. She liked colour very much, and flowers—especially perfumed flowers. When she arranged flowers for the house she would carefully select just the right vase. (I counted her vases one day and found that

Selma Ahrens, aged 17.

she had a hundred.) The arranging of them would be done with care and attention and, instead of being a chore, it would suddenly seem like a celebration.

She had a special talent for choosing presents, too. One Christmas when I was quite young she arrived with Japanese silk sunshades. Doris, my eldest sister, got a red one, brilliantly red when the sun shone through it; Audrey's was a vivid blue, Elsie's was pale egg-shell blue with mauve lozenge shapes patterned over it, and mine was purple, rich and beautiful, with a border of pale pink carnations. As the weather was very hot, we put them up immediately and strolled around in pairs chatting to each other in an offhand way as though we always walked about in the sun with parasols. I longed to be seen by someone who knew me, some classmates, for example, or indeed anyone at all who might be dazzled by my gorgeous sunshade. But, as we lived on a farm at the end of a private road, this was most unlikely.

When she was eighty-three she had a stroke. After this she was unable to speak and she died a few weeks later. I don't think she would have wanted to live any longer in this very diminished state. For one who had always been so quick to give expression to feelings it must have been very difficult.

Her special qualities lived on, because we would often say, 'Wouldn't Auntie have enjoyed this?' So it seems to me that if a human being has this precious gift—the gift of enthusiasm—and gives expression to it, there is a flow-on effect, bringing pleasure to others. Perhaps one of the most important things we can do is to enjoy life.

1940s
Ingenuity
~
Lesley Ferguson

It is the final year at Karori Primary School for me; our family is complete again after the war and although life is beginning to change, neighbourhood events are carrying on as usual.

Richard and Jamie have had a good idea to make some money. Richard's father is manager of the produce market in town, and sometimes Richard is taken down to hear the auctioneers racing through the bidding on the masses of fruit, vegetables, and flowers on the floor. It sounds exciting and very busy.

Post war. Saturday morning meeting place in Granny's summer house.

Jamie lives next door to Richard, in a house we love to visit as it is so modern. Most of the houses have gardens which are quite large. Ours is a bit smaller—it was divided off from my grandparents' place. Granny's place is separated from Richard's house by a row of cabbage trees which stand huge and untidy, dropping their sword leaves all over the spreading lawns, and between these trees runs a hedge of dusty Eely Agnes and prickly, glossy holly. Richard's father, Bill, is always cutting their other hedge, sticky escallonia. It towers up above us, and is always swallowing balls, each time we play in the garden.

All the gardens connect, with gaps for missing gates and fence palings (long since removed) and holes in hedges. Even the dustmen know their way around the gardens, to Granny's disapproval. The children in the neighbourhood can travel unseen, almost, from house to house—so we are all keen stalkers and hunters. How Richard and Jamie avoided being seen when they carried out the Good Idea, though, was baffling to us, and the adults too.

This Saturday morning, Mother is talking to a neighbour, Ann McKay, who says that young Richard and Jamie have been to the door selling bags of potatoes, nice fresh ones. 'Taking after his father, I expect,' she laughs. Mother thinks it is unusual, and that Bill would not really like his son selling paper bags of potatoes around the neighbourhood—it wasn't as if it was for the cubs, or fundraising, was it?

Mother goes down across the garden to see Monica. Monica says, 'Have a cuppa with me, in the sun. Look at the nice potatoes I've just bought from Richard—only sixpence, too. Probably some of Bill's stock.'

Often on sunny Saturday mornings the family gathers for a cuppa at Granny's summerhouse, sitting on cushions on great concrete sun-baked flagstones, and we listen to the adults talk. It is fascinating. This time they are laughing about Richard's ingenuity. I don't know why my brother and I don't have any to talk about—ingenuity, that is.

A short time later Monica comes up to our place. She is angry. Face white, mouth a straight line, and her brown eyes, usually twinkling, are cold and dark.

'*Someone* has dug up my potatoes, the lot! My vegetable garden is a real mess. All that hard work . . . who, who would do such a thing to me?'

Then the penny dropped. Silence, and we all stared at each other. 'Oh,' Monica gulped, 'I have just paid for my *own* potatoes!'

1930s
Giant Unseen
~
Heather Williams

FIRST VISITATION, PALMERSTON NORTH, 1931:
The house writhed, creaking and groaning as it was tortured in the hands of this visiting giant, whose power was such that it threw my parents from side to side of the long passage as they struggled to reach my sister and me standing in our bedroom doorway. For us two- and three-year-olds it was hard to understand why this giant was shaking our house so violently. Where had he come from? What did he want? After what seemed a long time we were gathered up in our parents' arms and carried outside into the big back yard just as the chimney came crashing down. Soon, the giant decided he had done enough damage and, with one last shiver, ceased his work. Where had he gone? Would he come back?

SECOND VISITATION, ASHHURST, 1942:
The giant was back! He announced his coming with a gentle rumble but his footsteps were enough, at first, to set the water tanks jiggling on their stands. Then, as his pace increased, the jiggling of the tanks assumed a frantic dance, until it seemed they must surely topple off their stands. The water sloshing about inside created a strange kind of music modulated according to how full the tanks were.

As there were three tanks near our bedroom, we were again evacuated, this time on to the tennis court. Not a breath of wind, not a sound out here on the lawn. The night was black and silent. We stood mesmerised, watching the tall black pines swaying in an arc against a black and starless sky. What evil was afoot on such a night?

Beneath our feet the ground rippled, in a sea of waves running the length of the tennis court—one such wave forever frozen on the service line. It was eerie to watch the giant move so gracefully, so silently. It was as if he was controlling an orchestra, with baton pointed first in one direction and then in the other.

With a final frenzy of movement the giant passed on, leaving the pines waving slowly, rhythmically, while the melody of the tanks quietened to a whisper . . .

1930s
Paradise Gained

~

Joyce Harrison

It was my father's idea to hook Mum's canoe above the mantelpiece of our new bach. I marvelled at the suggestion—it would set this place up as Mum's new Fiji. Her nostalgia for the Islands haunted my earlier years—it was almost as if I had been born beneath the rustle of coconut palms and the glow of the tropical moon. She sang me to sleep with *Isa Lei*, the Fijian lament, and those longing cadences are woven into my memory. She would play it from the sheet music whose front cover had a frilly red flower beside a smiling golliwog head.

She would take down one of her shells from the dresser for me to pore over, absorbing the patterns set deep into their glassy backs. On the top they were like little curled up animals, but underneath two rows of teeth firmly closed on whatever secrets were within. These shells were not friendly, like the fibre fan. They could not be bent or scratched, or even drawn upon. They had never been born or made and would go on for ever, never wearing out or even changing, taking their strange beauty with them.

My favourite treasure was the model outrigger canoe, longer than my arm, its dark wood gleaming with diamonds of inlaid shell. If in the right mood Mother would bring out its long box, pull back the tissue wrapping and allow me to finger the points of the tiny, perfect oars, and be filled with wonder, thinking of this little ship travelling so far from its magical home.

Long before I could read the captions, the tapa cloth-covered photo album appeared. Mum turned the black pages and I saw shiny pictures of groups of men and women clustered laughing on the beach in black knee-length bathing togs, ladies in long white dresses and wide-brimmed hats swinging tennis racquets, or Fijian men in tight white skirts with pointy zig-zag hems. She would tell me of the excitement when the navy was due in port, and about the preparations for balls at the Grand Pacific, which lasted all night; of rafting weekends up lonely rivers, meeting a real cannibal chief, and trips with the resident judge to outlying villages where she took notes for him in clever shorthand. In between these adventures she was responsible for writing in shorthand everything said in the Parliament.

In the end she had to come back to New Zealand, and this created a problem for me . . . She had given up that paradise in order to have me, I thought. How could I make up for all that she had sacrificed for me? It could be argued that she was now looking after Dad as well, but he could surely have looked after himself; but me, I couldn't even have got to be alive without her help. In time I was old enough to work out that she hadn't come home to produce me, that a year had elapsed between her return in the mid 1920s and her first meeting with Father, but the dilemma lingered. After all, living here on a hilltop section, house shaking in the southerlies, hard clay struggling to produce sparse ngaios, cabbage trees and hydrangeas, could seemingly in no way compensate for the brilliant flowers, the golden paw paws, the tiny lady's finger bananas she had left behind. Letters would arrive from time to time with colourful foreign stamps. There was no doubt about their origin. How could Dad and I match the sparkling company she had so obviously enjoyed?

I acquired Mum's awkward iron-framed tennis racquet when tall enough to wield it, and the other kids teased me because it was different. I silenced them by explaining that in the tropics wood and catgut rotted, and that my mother, a crack player, had ordered this one specially from New Zealand. I was loyal to that racquet, to the extent of declining the offer of a cousin's discard. Learning to play tennis with such cumbersome equipment didn't seem as hard as trying to replace the charms of an unseen land.

I was about eight when we bought our beach section and embarked on slashing and burning our way through mountains of South African boxthorn and sneezy lupins to make way for a tent, and a couple of years later a one-roomed bach. From our sand dune bank above the beach Mum pointed out that Kapiti was about the same distance from the mainland as was Bega, the island on which she had watched the firewalkers strolling over red hot stones.

Above the fireplace of our unlined bach the builders had added a large square of varnished pinex, as a finishing touch. Dad suggested this as an ideal place for displaying the stored canoe. Mum, who was surprisingly casual about the project, agreed and it was given a ceremonial unveiling. I proposed painting a mural below it—a tropical island scene, coconut palms along the side, little bures below and cowrie shells dotted about the golden sand. Mum did not enthuse. 'Why don't you paint a scene from around here?' she suggested, and she seemed to mean it.

After making a careful appraisal of the view from the top of our track I started painting: a cliff face like a brown waterfall to represent the Paekak hill on the right, then a green hillock with a Norfolk pine. On the left lay the sweeping curve of waves on the beach, and Kapiti set on the skyline, a little huddled, to squeeze it all in. Overhead, in my patchy blue sky there sailed, like a witch on a broomstick, the outrigger canoe. Around this point something must have opened my mother's eyes.

We are sitting together on the bank above the sea, and she is opening my eyes in return.

'I had a wonderful two years in Fiji, as you know,' she began, 'and as I may have told you [which she had, of course] they tried hard to persuade me to stay on and join the permanent staff. One more year and I would have had a trip to England on full pay, and from then on an overseas trip every two years. But what I was really wanting at that time was what I've got now—a happy family and a home of my own.'

The following summer I was given my first brand new tennis racquet. Real smart it was, white and gold and light as a feather.

Independence

1950s /1980s
Breakfast
~
Kay Carter

I *like* cold toast! Cold crunchy toast with butter and homemade marmalade is for me the essence of breakfast, but my first breakfast memories are of the taste of—was it Granola? It is a taste memory that I have not been able to recapture.

As a child preparing for school I remember my mother being up early to take the coarse Vi-Max out of the haybox where it had been cooking overnight after being slowly brought to the boil the night before. It was then put on to the Moffat stove and stirred so that it didn't catch on the bottom of the pot. Don and I dressed by the heater that lived under the big open legs of the stove. It was a wonderful way to start the day. Porridge with golden syrup and clotted cream that, in Dad's words, 'You could sole your boots with.' Afterwards a piece of toast with honey from Dad's hives.

Boarding school breakfasts were quite different: a large hall-like room full of chattering girls aged from seven to fifteen years, ten to a table and sitting on forms, except for the supervising prefect at the top of the table. The prefects were watched in their turn by the staff seated on their raised platform. Breakfast was an ordered affair with plenty of cold toast and marmalade and honey in bowls that could be replenished by the prefects from five-pound tins in the big kitchen.

I moved to a Post Office hostel in Wellington when I was seventeen, and there the dining-room tables for four had white tablecloths and the cutlery was set out for us. We ate our toast to the sound of the trams as they banged and clattered their way from the terminus.

Years of feeding my young children meant breakfast 'on the hoof' and more often than not cold toast. This routine was broken one year by breakfasts on board ship—a very grown-up affair because the children, after an early breakfast sitting, were left in the nursery for the day. Mothers were free to be with other adults and enjoy the atmosphere and excitement of sailing to the other side of the world. (There was also the anxiety of anticipation: meeting the in-laws in Ireland for the first time.)

My Irish sisters-in-law were late risers, wondrously disorganised and at breakfast time always rushing for the bus. There was never time for breakfast; just a piece of cold toast as they hurried down the street.

I have memories of many and varied breakfasts, from the enormous smorgasbords in American hotels to the Polish hotel at Gdynia where we were supplied with hot water—add your own choice of tea bag—and scrambled eggs and bacon served in the tiny pan in which they had been cooked. In 1983 that was a luxury breakfast; most of the locals would have had no more than tea and black bread.

In Greece we enjoyed rolls and jam, madeira cake and real orange juice. We sat in the rooftop restaurant of our central Athens hotel overlooking the Plaka and the Acropolis. In Germany there were crisp crunchy buns, lots of sausage, fresh soft herb cheese, coffee and, if you wanted it, some rich fruit cake. Danish pastries in Copenhagen, and in Japan our ryokan served many little dishes of pickled vegetables, hot bean soup into which a raw egg was mixed, rice and green tea. We sat on the floor in our own separate tiny breakfast room with a glass wall framing an equally small but exquisite Japanese garden.

The most energising breakfast is the full cooked English breakfast. I have enjoyed many such feasts at Pauline and Stephen Gatley's bed and breakfast establishment near Gatwick airport—a big plate of bacon, eggs, tomato, chips, baked beans, black pudding and fried bread, after cereal and followed by tea and toast. That would last me most of the day.

But best of all is the leisurely breakfast of tea and toast we now enjoy together in retirement. The bread that Bill bakes, any of his varieties, is very tasty with homemade marmalade—when it is cold and crunchy toast.

1940s
Mac
~
Lesley Ferguson

'Let me show you our new residence,' said Mac, patting the seat beside him. I clambered up into the cab of the truck, watched dejectedly from our kitchen window by my mother. I enjoyed the feeling of power and elevation from that truck seat, as much as my parents disliked it, and the driver. We churned down the street, and charged across the city in high style, while Mac, whose proper name I cannot recall, explained that his mother and father, newly arrived from England, had had difficulty in finding a moderately priced house.

Now Mac was great, one of those people who could do anything he put his mind to, and it seemed that he was the stuff that pioneer New Zealanders were made of. Not, however, a quality my parents could see. He could ski superbly, which in those days was notable, he could dance so well, and he enjoyed socialising, though with a different crowd—which widened my horizons! He could be bossy—'Don't wear makeup'—arrogant, and organising. But we had fun, and outings with Mac were interesting, especially when we went to the International Club events.

'It's a wonderful address, has the most superb view in Wellington, and it's affordable,' he laughed, ' . . . hold on,' and we dived across Oriental Parade to grind up Roseneath hill, fearless of other traffic on that bendy route. We stopped alongside St Barnabas Church, where several of my former school friends had properly spent time on Sundays.

We stepped down from the cab and I looked around with fresh interest. A nice area all right. Trust Mac! He headed towards a scruffy right-of-way beside the church and I could hear the chuckle in his voice, a sort of one-upmanship tone, as he said, 'The view—a million-pound view—just look.' Distant mountains to the north, beyond the Hutt Valley, a southerly-scuffed harbour scattered with Saturday yachties was spread before us. Directly in front of us, down a broken drive, was a tumbledown old cottage, clumps of couch grass and a battered paling fence alongside a playground.

'The other condemned house was demolished,' said Mac. 'Developers are going to build a block of flats here.'

Mr and Mrs Mac came out to welcome me, buckets, cloths, hammers and nails left for the moment. They showed me around. A sunken worn step, minute kitchen, a scratched and forgettable sink with califont for water supply, a low and dingy back room used for laundry and bathroom where just outside I could hear the water tank dripping into soggy ground. The house smelt musty, old and mouldy. But the pioneering spirit won, and each horrendous repair was enthusiastically described to me. The uneven passage, bulgy walls, different levels, broken floors—all led to The View from the 'front' room where we found boxes to sit on while Mrs Mac collected mugs and boiled water on the gas stove.

Mac wasn't one for sitting over the tea cups for long and soon became restless. 'I'm going to show you the garden and the cliff path,' he said, escaping with me.

Mrs Mac went back to her cleaning, but cast an eye at the lowering sun. 'We need the water fixed, don't forget, and we do need your help.' She was so cheerful, and undaunted. It hadn't occurred to her to question their work on the condemned cottage. Mr Mac was attacking some boards. He had keen blue eyes, very twinkly. Mac told me his father had been a bobsleigh driver once, and he seemed very dashing.

We chatted for a moment or two before departing, and Mrs Mac wistfully mentioned the way they spent Saturdays 'at home'. 'We used to go dancing—Mr Mac is a smashing dancer—and the whole family would go, and Mac's girlfriend, the one he left in England.' That's a safe distance, I thought.

'She was a beautiful girl,' said Mrs Mac, regretfully, 'Lovely hair, lovely hands, lovely parts . . . ' (I can recall that expression still.) 'We did have smashing times.'

As we charged home across the city, my large hands and long feet glared at me silently in the cab of the truck. Mac used the wartime trick of saving fuel by coasting down the hills with the engine out of gear, and smartly engaging gears as power was needed—it was hard on the brakes.

The Saturday chores had been done in our tree-sheltered garden, and my family were relieved to see me step down from that truck, safe home.

It was some time before I decided to tell them the details of the old house, and the state of it. When I did, they failed to see the glamour of the pioneering spirit, but asked Mac and his family home for tea.

I have since remembered why we all called him Mac—it was because his parents called him CLARENCE!

1940s
Messages
~
Kay Carter

My life today is tempered by strong messages received from my childhood, messages about how a girl or young lady should behave, think and what her expectations of life might be. They came probably from my parents, but also from the attitudes of those around me: my cousins, Sunday school teachers, school teachers and fellow pupils at a country school.

In the 1940s a girl under twelve could have only one goal that I can recall: to be a wife and mother. To be a nurturer and take care of others. In the games we played these concepts were evident. At school and at home on the farm we built playhouses under the trees. There was a row of tall lawsoniana trees at school which the boys climbed. But young ladies 'didn't climb trees'. We made rooms underneath. We brought curtains from home, anything that could be strung as a room divider. We made brooms with branches and swept the hard dirt floors—a further early recognition of the future exercise of housekeeping skills.

I was instructed not to eat in the street; it was 'not ladylike'—and one did *not* chew gum! The only time this was permissible was on a long car journey when my mother thought it helped prevent car sickness. On one occasion, though, it found an alternative use—to block a punctured petrol tank.

Once a week my brother and I had music lessons at the local convent. This meant being collected by our parents after school and driven to lessons. While we were with the nuns our parents had messages to do, and our occasional treat as we waited in the car for them was to buy from Collin's Bakery a quarter loaf of fresh white bread. We always had wholemeal or brown bread at home and white bread was a real treat. We used to sit in the car and pull this bread to pieces from the soft white 'kissing crust'. We hollowed out the loaf and eventually ate the crisp crunchy crust. Another real treat at that time was to be allowed to buy, at the cost of 11 pence, a tin of condensed milk which, when boiled in water for some time, thickened and caramelised.

At an all-girls high school very little thought was given to today's range of possible careers. We had no options presented to us. I did not want to be a nurse or a teacher, and work in an office didn't appeal either, but that is what I ended up doing. The messages at school were more subliminal. We were so sheltered and naive. We were isolated from the rest of the world, cut off, allowed home at holiday time with one *exeat* a term. When we did go out we found a world for which we were totally unprepared.

I was so shy I could not speak to anyone—or, as my father said, I 'wouldn't say boo to a goose'. I had many instilled messages: 'Don't wear your heart on your sleeve,' and, 'A lady is not impulsive, isn't aggressive or competitive and definitely does not show strong emotions.'

I learned through years of experience that to get angry over things beyond my control hurt me more than it hurt anyone else and there were no 'Brownie points' to be gained in that. I definitely could not give expression to my emotions, my needs or wants, thinking it was bad and unladylike to think of myself. 'A lady is always in control and never seeks power for herself.' 'A lady always backs down.' This brings to mind that although in my teenage years I thoroughly enjoyed swimming and the hours of training that involved, I did not like racing. Since we were taught as small children to be seen and not heard, and not to stand out, is it any wonder that we did not ever consider our own potential?

A woman's role was to be a caretaker, to respond to the feelings and needs of others, to respond without negative reaction, to be strong and caring for others. If you did not feel well, you should get all your jobs done today in case you felt worse tomorrow. That was one of the messages that surfaced when I was bringing up four young children. In those days I disliked taking medication, and I remember my mother saying, 'If you have a headache, take a Disprin for the benefit of the children if not for yourself.'

Sadly there is no guarantee that doing good for other people leads to feeling good within one's own self. I was cocooned within my own home and family, thinking of being good, doing the right things, but not even considering feeling good within or about myself.

As time progressed I assumed the blame for the problems within the family, thinking that if I worked harder I would remove the reasons for my husband's drinking. There was too much trying to do everything and too much of the caring, nurturing woman.

I had had no preparation for relationships and my assumption was that if my husband behaved badly there was something that I could do about it. I catered to his every whim, but the right answer today would be the wrong answer tomorrow. Everything revolved around him and the children. I cooked the meals he liked, kept the children quiet, took care of household responsibilities, went out to work and took in boarders to build up the family's income. It was many years before I accepted that I was not responsible for his actions.

It has been incredibly difficult to sort the wheat from the chaff and to reject those messages that I do not agree with. I love being impulsive and doing impulsive things and I really enjoy the feeling—is it of power?—when I stand and address a big audience. Today I walk tall and stand tall. In the past the downside of my height was that I was always at the end of the line, often last.

Life is full of the messages we are given by those around us. They are both positive and negative. For eighteen years I lived with alcoholism and was told by my husband that I was useless, that I could do nothing worthwhile. I was told that I couldn't write anything that made sense, that I couldn't cook, and so many other negative messages. My second husband is totally the opposite and he encourages me to do so many things, and go out on my own and find out what I can and what I want to do. I am finding so many challenges I can willingly accept.

1940s
How Nice to be Free
~
Rachelle Calkoen

Just after the war I took a job as secretary to a captain of the Dutch army. Our headquarters were in Groningen, a university town in the north of the Netherlands. We did a lot of travelling to old army camps, to take stock. I found it very enjoyable. We had a good car, which at that time was a real luxury, and we often took hitchhikers with us. The trains weren't going yet and people had no cars, and no tyres for their bikes, if they had bikes at all, because most of them had been confiscated by the Germans during the five years of occupation.

One day, driving out of Groningen past lots of hitchhikers, my boss said, 'Today we won't take any nurses, military personnel or nice young girls, because they will always get a car; but that man there will have trouble getting a lift.' And he stopped in front of a shabbily dressed old man and told him to get in the back. The man was absolutely delighted and kept on talking, making comments about the weather, the countryside, and several times uttered sentences such as, 'Isn't it nice to be free?' or 'How wonderful to be free again!'—sentiments that we shared, of course, but when the captain elaborated on the German defeat, it became clear that our passenger wasn't talking about the Germans at all, but that he had just come out of prison.

'I'm a pickpocket, you see,' he told us proudly. We had promised to take him to a town 200 km away, and my boss thought, 'Good heavens, in that time he'll have taken my wallet, my watch, my chequebook, and goodness knows what else!' He felt most uncomfortable, and decided that the quicker we could be rid of this bloke the better. He put his foot down and raced away, far exceeding the speed limit.

It wasn't long before a traffic cop caught up with us. Sirens screaming, he came alongside and motioned us to stop. The little black book came out of his pocket and all the relevant information was duly written down.

'You'll hear from us,' were his parting words, and we could go.

The captain was furious. 'It's all your fault!' he fumed at the old man. 'If we hadn't picked you up, and if you hadn't told us you were a pickpocket, I wouldn't have driven so fast, and I wouldn't have to pay a fine!'

The old man laughed. 'But you don't have to,' he said. 'One good turn is worth another!' And with that he produced the policeman's black book.

1940s
By Wind and Water
~
Heather Williams

'Hike! Hike!' came the command from the skipper as we strained our bodies as far out as possible over the gunwale, trying to keep the twelve-foot Idle Along yacht *San Toy* from capsizing. The wind hums in the rigging, the heavy cotton sails full and taut. Forward, strong hands, knuckles whitened with the pressure, grasp the jib sheet, while the skipper controls the main sheet with one hand, the other holding strongly on to the tiller. Blue eyes scan the sea and watch the pennant at the top of the mast to read the wind as it comes screaming down the gully to dump in the bay scurrying fingers of high-pressure air blasting in all directions. Wild sheets of spray fling over boat and crew, cold as ice, as it drenches our faces and trickles down our necks. The dreaded Kio Bay buoy approaches, the site where many a good yachtie was sure to capsize at some stage.

'Stand by for about!' The command rising above the wind is followed a few seconds later with 'Leeo!'—the skipper judging a brief lull in the wind, time to change tack. The leeward jib sheet is released with a quick snap from the cleat, sails flap protestingly, the boom swings over with a crack, and another gust comes roaring down the gully. 'Hike!

Hike!' Bodies strain, pushing hard down the weather gunwale, but to no avail. This time the wind has its way and we are over in the cold, unforgiving sea. A melee of sight, sound and senses, one mighty chorus of voices, wind and water. Bulky kapok-filled life jackets keep us afloat.

The men soon swing the bow into the wind, one standing on the centre plate—the keel, to centreboarders—the other straining and pulling on the weather gunwale to force the yacht to lift her mast and sails out of the water and upright again. It seems an eternity. The wind still screams and the yacht, now righted, wallows heavily, the cockpit awash with water. Sails flap madly, sending sheets of water into the air as the wind furiously slaps and shakes them unmercifully. The men scramble on board and empty the boat with a heavy four-sided wooden hand pump that sucks and spews the water back to its rightful place.

Among the crew is a shy young girl unfamiliar with the art of sailing, every part of it entirely foreign to her—including the pair of men's trousers, borrowed from the skipper. She grasps the traveller on the stern of the boat with one hand, the other clutching desperately at the trousers which threaten at any moment to become but a memory.

The cockpit is finally empty, things made shipshape, and then! Then! the shy cold, wet, bedraggled young girl is grasped unceremoniously by the seat of the offending trousers and dumped in the bottom of the boat.

Hurriedly the jib and main sheets are pulled taut once more and we are off, scudding along in the sheer joy of strength and skill against the force of wind and sea.

And the young girl? That was me—I had been well and truly initiated. Four months later I married the skipper—Yippee!

1940s
Riding on the Engine
~
Joyce Harrison

We piled off the Limited with all the other passengers. We didn't bother with the rush for railway tea. It was the first time either of us had been on holiday without adults, and it was exciting enough just looking around. It was then we spotted Mr Oldham, who had recently spoken to our class at varsity about the country's railways, emphasising the special status of the Limited as the biggest and fastest of all the trains

Independence

running between Wellington and Auckland. Such was his status in the railways that we hesitated to presume an acquaintance.

That was until I surprised us both by suggesting that we ask him if he could arrange for us to have a ride in the engine. Pauline jumped at the idea, so we wandered over and reminded Mr Oldham of his interesting talk to the students. He seemed pleased to chat, so we gradually worked around to our outrageous request. The senior official turned solemn. He was sorry but this was strictly against the regulations. We were of course not surprised and returned to casual subjects, Mr Oldman nevertheless continuing to look thoughtful. When the warning bell clanged and passengers started piling back on to the train, he said to us quickly: 'I'll come along to your carriage just before the next stop, but don't talk about it.'

Paekakariki Station. Photo courtesy Paekakariki Rail and Heritage Museum and Paekakariki Surf Club.

As the train rattled through the countryside the windows darkened. We watched the carriage door with twittering excitement. Eventually it opened. There was our fellow conspirator. We were smartly out in the aisle and through the carriage. At the next stop, he hustled us down the steps and along the platform. The engine loomed huge and black, with steam hissing out all over it. I was scared by now, and worried for Mr Oldham; but he was more like a schoolboy on a spree. When the bell clanged we were quickly hoisted up the metal steps onto the cab. A little iron gate banged shut. We were given some sort of introduction to the driver and fireman, most of it lost in the general din. These men were clearly none too happy about our presence, even with their boss alongside. However, they stationed us on little wooden seats attached to the back wall of the cab, one on each side. Then the hissing turned into chuffing and we jolted off into the night.

The sudden violent swaying and shuddering had us hanging on tight, each to our own little iron gate. We were soon careering through the night, hair flying out behind, and showers of bright sparks floating by, high above in the billows of smoke. As signals and telegraph poles flashed past, the men tossed bits of information to us, again mostly lost in the uproar and the wind.

What if we hit a cow? The driver was leaning out from the side, watching the way ahead—although now it was completely dark but for the twin slivers of light on the rails. But why worry? These sturdy fellows must know what they're doing, and they'd be killed too if we flew off the tracks . . . We swung madly round a curve. We gasped in amazement as the fireman swung open the round furnace door on a scorching red cavern. He shovelled in coal from a bin alongside him and slammed the heavy door. This was really living!

I was half-disappointed and half-relieved when the engine began to slow. Mr Oldham directed the men to stop just past the station lights. We were shepherded down quickly to solid ground. Mr Oldham smiled when we tried to muster up our thanks. Again he turned serious. Very few women had ever travelled in the cab of the Limited. Not a word to anyone!

It seemed a great shame to have to keep quiet about our experience, but I would probably have kept my part of the deal forever—had not the memory of it all come rushing back the other night when I came across the obituary notice for Frank Oldham. My thanks to him for giving us one of the highlights of our youth.

1950s
Good Taste
~
Lesley Ferguson

First there was Doug, her brother's friend. He hunted, tramped, and motorbiked. They played golf together. As Jenny got to know him she discovered speed thrills, aching exhausted muscles, air shots and clean hits. Besides being a good sport, Doug, she discovered, was a very convenient partner at balls. Tall and freshcut, preceded by the smell of—Knight's Castile? —he would bounce around the ballroom floor, all attention and enthusiasm.

His real love was for outdoor adventures, however, and he became increasingly 'adventurous' around the city limits when they lost their golf balls in the pine trees . . . They eventually went their separate ways, she to agricultural college, he to study engineering elsewhere. She told him she didn't want to marry him, but they remained friends, as did their families—polite but not familiar.

Then there was Dave, a fellow Massey student, wild but gentle. His deeds were talked (whispered) about. Whose tyres had scoured the carefully tended grass around the plane trees up the drive? Who put glue in the boys' Brylcreme? He became the star of her sky as he hummed 'Don't let the stars get in your eyes . . . don't let the moon break your heart . . . ' Heady stuff for Jenny, from one so gruff and ostensibly girl-shy.

Occasionally, after late swot sessions in the library, they went to town for supper and muffins—when he thought no one would observe his friendliness with a girl. 'Oh Happy Day' was their theme song. From time to time he gave her lifts to sports meetings. There were delicious moments when they made up a supper foursome with a friend of his and his girlfriend. Jenny observed and absorbed so much: the way he walked with a horsey old farmer's roll, dragging the cuffs of his trousers, the way he smiled, his enthusiasm for recorded music and hi-fi equipment. There were times when they'd take a more rural route home, cuddling tentatively in the car against the unromantic background of cows munching beyond the wire fence.

Time moved them on different tracks, she to work in a plant nursery, to dream and wait for letters; he to a South Island university. Letters did come, infrequent, amusing, treasured. Among the accounts of social doings and university capers was mention of a Fiona McLeod, leading to a reluctant thought ' . . . Don't let the moon break your heart . . .'

The University Tournament came around, with the excitement of competition, and meeting old friends—screaming good fun and sodden parties. Dave was there, but distant, engrossed with his events on the rifle range and his many friends. Jenny suddenly found she could no longer shoot clean goals; her clothes looked awful and she had put on weight—too much bread and dairy factory cheese. Life had lost its zest.

Holiday time, students back in town . . . and a call from Doug, fresh off the inter-island ferry. 'Come over and see us. Mum's been baking. I'll come over on the bike and collect you.'

'Take our car,' Jenny's father offered with rare alacrity.

'Too late, he's on his way, but thanks,' said Jenny.

Once again Jenny huddled in the pillion seat, gripping with her knees, hands planted firmly on his bony hips, as they took off into the slicing wind.

The Brown house in Berhampore was one of a row of 1920s two-storied houses. Dark rooms, steep stairs, lace curtains, a house full of boots, packs, guns, and dogs. Doug's sombre-eyed father was settled impassively in a dark corner of the photo-crowded living room. He was small and spare with a high-domed forehead. His brooding monosyllabic presence cast a tension over the room.

Large as life, with a gale of lively chatter and cheery greetings, Mrs Brown wheeled in the tea trolley. Jenny was torn between good manners, weight sensitivity, and simple delight at the amazing load of goodies on the trolley. It was always the same with Mrs B. In the end fear of disappointing the cook—who had produced two kinds of Fielders fluffy cream sponges, melting moments, Anzac biscuits and fruit cake—won again. Jenny and Doug cradled their hot cups of tea in their chilled hands while the lively chatter surrounded them and apparently weighed on Mr Brown, as he sank deeper into his chair.

Mrs Brown, buxom, strong and overpoweringly energetic, talked about her riotous garden, the cuttings she'd struck, and the tobacco seeds she planned to sow. Enough to make a horticulturist feel unnecessary! Her luxuriant harvest-gold hair was swept into a loose knot with elusive hairpins, so wisps escaped and framed her eager face. Jenny helped with the tea dishes and then went out with Doug into the flourishing back garden to view progress and chat.

'Well,' said Doug, 'I have a new girlfriend, you'll be pleased to know.

She's a great outdoor girl . . . her father's a farmer from Te Aroha. Her name is Kathy . . . Kathy McLeod.'

'What a coincidence,' said Jenny, sourly.

'Yes,' said Doug, 'her sister Fiona is going out with another ex-boyfriend of yours, Dave.' (Ouch!) Their mother has heard of you, and she's quite impressed with your taste in boys. She says to tell you that she has two other daughters . . . '

1950s
Red Dress
~
Kay Carter

'Take that back at once!' my mother said, in a very determined there-will-be-no-discussion tone of voice. Up to that time I had made my own clothes, taking over from my mother who had been a seamstress and a very patient teacher.

In 1953 there was not much spare money to buy clothes. They were much more expensive in relation to income at that time. This had been my first purchase. Well, it wasn't even that. It was still possible to take

Kay ready for her first day at work.

a garment from a store 'on approval', and I had been delighted to arrange to do this during the week.

On the Friday I had climbed aboard the commuter bus to Cambridge with my treasure in my bag, carefully wrapped in tissue paper. This was after my week's work at Federated Farmers as the office junior.

I had had a very safe, secure and happy childhood on my parents' farm in the Waikato. They had showed us many places on our summer holidays. But now here I was with my first job in Hamilton. After paying my Monday-to-Friday board of £1 10s in Hunter Street, Hamilton, I had saved enough money and was able, as I thought, to buy my first dress.

'Nice girls don't wear red!' had been my mother's next statement.

On Monday, my ego flattened, I obediently returned the dress. I felt really deflated. My first attempt to make an independent purchase had been shattered.

'What is so different about red?' I thought. 'And what did she mean by "nice girls"?'

1950s
Wedding Day

~

Shirley Dobbs Signal

Our wedding day was a kaleidoscope, a time warp, a day of enchantment, a day when everything was wonderful, or hilarious, or magical, or exactly how I'd always dreamed it should be.

It was a million things: managing not to cry when the *Lohengrin* Wedding March started up, because I had suddenly remembered my mascara wasn't waterproof; it was not minding when I received not one but two revolting horseshoes; gazing at my brand-new husband as he delivered a polished and witty speech, and realising yet again what an incredibly talented and wonderful man I had married!

It was my father deciding that we should have two signs over two sections of the Reception Lounge: 'Goodies' and 'Baddies'—the Goodies for my husband's relations, who didn't drink alcohol, the Baddies for us, who all downed champagne with the best of them.

It was the beautiful wedding service, conducted by a minister who sounded as if he really believed in what he was doing.

It was dancing round the garden with my father in the early morning, singing, 'Dis is da Day—Dis is da Day . . . '

It was my upstairs bedroom at home, with all my girlfriends preparing me for Going Away, those already married giving me advice.

It was finding that over the last few days I had lost so much weight that my mother had to sew temporary extra seams in my Going Away outfit. (She did it with stocking mending thread, and it was still intact five years later.)

It was the traditional cutting of the wedding cake, and finding that the knife wouldn't go through the icing! (We have a series of photos in which the knife blade ends up practically at right angles to the handle, and we end up in near hysterics.)

It was the surprise visit our wedding party made to a friend in St Helen's Hospital who had just had her fifth child. As we left, my new husband waved to the assembled staff and patients, and called, 'See you next year!' I blushed, and thought him deliciously wicked.

It was one of my father's friends at the reception stuffing his pockets full of bananas—why, I wonder?—and then forgetting all about them until he fell back into the seat of the taxi . . .

It was finding the extra-large haul of chicken bones and fruit skins in the two large Chinese vases which graced the floor of our lounge.

It was my tenor husband and his baritone friend singing the duet from the first act of *The Pearl Fishers*—and getting into the spirit of the thing so magnificently that the bridegroom had to be dragged away from the piano to join his bride on their honeymoon.

It was the wonderful hamper packed for us by the caterers (neither of us had eaten a thing to speak of during the day).

And our wedding day ended with the bride and groom, alone at last in their caravan, toasting each other and their future in champagne and chocolate sultana pasties!

1940s
Hitchhiking
~
Jeannette Hunter

In the summer of 1948 I finished the Montessori teachers' course and got a job in a Montessori preschool, starting in September after the summer holidays.

Chel and I had decided to go on a hitchhiking vacation through Belgium, France and Switzerland. That this might be dangerous for two girls didn't enter our heads, nor even our fearful mother's. Cars did not travel that fast because motorways didn't exist, apart from a few in Germany built by Hitler for military transport. It was easy to get a ride, especially from truck drivers who liked company on their long hauls.

At coffee, lunch or dinner stops we would offer to buy them something, but I can't remember that offer ever being accepted. On the contrary, they always invited us for a drink or something to eat, which sometimes led to difficulties: we were not used to the many glasses of wine the French people drank with (or without) their meals. Our hosts would refill our glasses, urging us to drink up.

One day our truckies invited us to a really excellent meal with, of course, the usual accompaniment of wine. I was pleased when we got to the coffee, as I felt somewhat lightheaded. But whoops! With the coffee a good glass of cognac arrived.

'Just pour it into your coffee,' advised our generous hosts. As they talked with Chel I tipped out my glass surreptitiously under my chair, but Chel, seeing my glass empty, did as she was told. It was unlucky for me that the floor was made of dark tiles, which showed up the big puddle I had made.

After all that drink we stopped in a forest for a 'comfort stop'. Chel got back in the cabin and before I could reach it, the truck drove off! She had the presence of mind to turn off the key. 'Just a bit of fun,' they said, but we were not so sure.

A few days later we got a lift in a jeep. It did not take long to notice that the driver had drunk rather too much. We asked to be let out but no, he'd take us to the next town for sure. Before we got there, however, we had to squeeze ourselves out of the back of the jeep, which had nose dived into a deep ditch.

Our finances, by that time, had dwindled to next to nothing so we wanted to get as quickly as possible to Geneva where Jeanne-Laure, our former Nanny and family friend, had some Swiss francs for us.

We were very lucky to be given a ride by a Monsieur Pougolas who was going to Geneva for a meeting. He took us over the mountains on a scenic route instead of going the quickest way, although he later told us he was in a bit of a hurry to get to his meeting on time. He even stopped at several vantage points to let us admire the view, and then raced on, tyres screaming, around the many hairpin bends. 'Are you afraid?' he asked. 'Do as I do—close your eyes on the corners.'

On hearing that we wouldn't have any Swiss money till the next day, he gave us some francs, ignoring our protests, and then left us near the Youth Hostel. He was a real sweetie. Later on we would call everyone we liked very much 'a Pougolas'.

The doors of the hostel were shut and nobody seemed to be home. We rang the bell several times before the Youth Hostel 'mother' opened the door and said, quite irritated, 'Oh, all these young people, I can't stand them!'

Several weeks later, we were finally making our way home from north-east France. It started to get dark—a difficult time to find a car willing to take us. So we asked the waiter, when he brought us something to eat, if he knew where the nearest Youth Hostel was. Our luck held—all along our trip we met pleasant people, trying to help us. This time it was the young man at the table next to ours, who asked why we wanted to go to a Youth Hostel.

'Well, it's the cheapest place to stay,' we said.

'My mother lives not far from here and she would put you up for nothing, I'm sure,' said our helpful neighbour. What a nice offer.

Off we went in his car, but we were not the only passengers. I had to share the back seat with a very big Alsatian dog. We drove and drove and drove, right up into the mountains. Had he not said that his mother lived close by? Yes, but he had a much better idea: he would take us to his house in the mountains, before going himself to his mother.

The house turned out to be a one-room hut deep in a forest. It had a wooden table and some chairs, two bunk beds and a couch. No electricity, so he put some water on a primus to make a hot drink before returning to civilisation. He stayed on and on, we didn't know how to get rid of him . . .

In the end he thought it was too late to go back, but never mind, we could sleep on the bunk beds while he would take the couch. Without a choice, that's what we did.

Both Chel and I crawled into our sleeping bags, taking off our shoes only, but we weren't going to close our eyes till we could hear him snoring. No such luck. He sat at the table talking with his big dog, who growled now and then in reply. The carbide lamp smelled and hissed and in its dim light I could see our host, glancing over at us, then getting up and taking his pistol and guns out of a cupboard. He started to take them to pieces, clean them and put them together again and polish them with care. By this time our host in my imagination had turned into a maniac and a murderer.

He got up again and came slowly towards our beds with his dog at his heels, sat down on Chel's bed and started to stroke her. That was the last straw. I quickly slipped down on the other side, wriggled into her sleeping bag, which really wasn't made to house two bodies.

We lay there quivering for a long while. Sleeping that night was out of the question, the tension in the hut was palpable! We were relieved when the man stormed out and asked us, when he came in again, to get ready as he wanted to get away early.

He dropped us on a main road at about 4.30 a.m. and we were lucky again: the truck driver was going all the way to Amsterdam.

We arrived home, a day earlier than planned, deciding not to tell Mother all of our adventures; and I made up my mind not to do any more hitchhiking.

Family Life

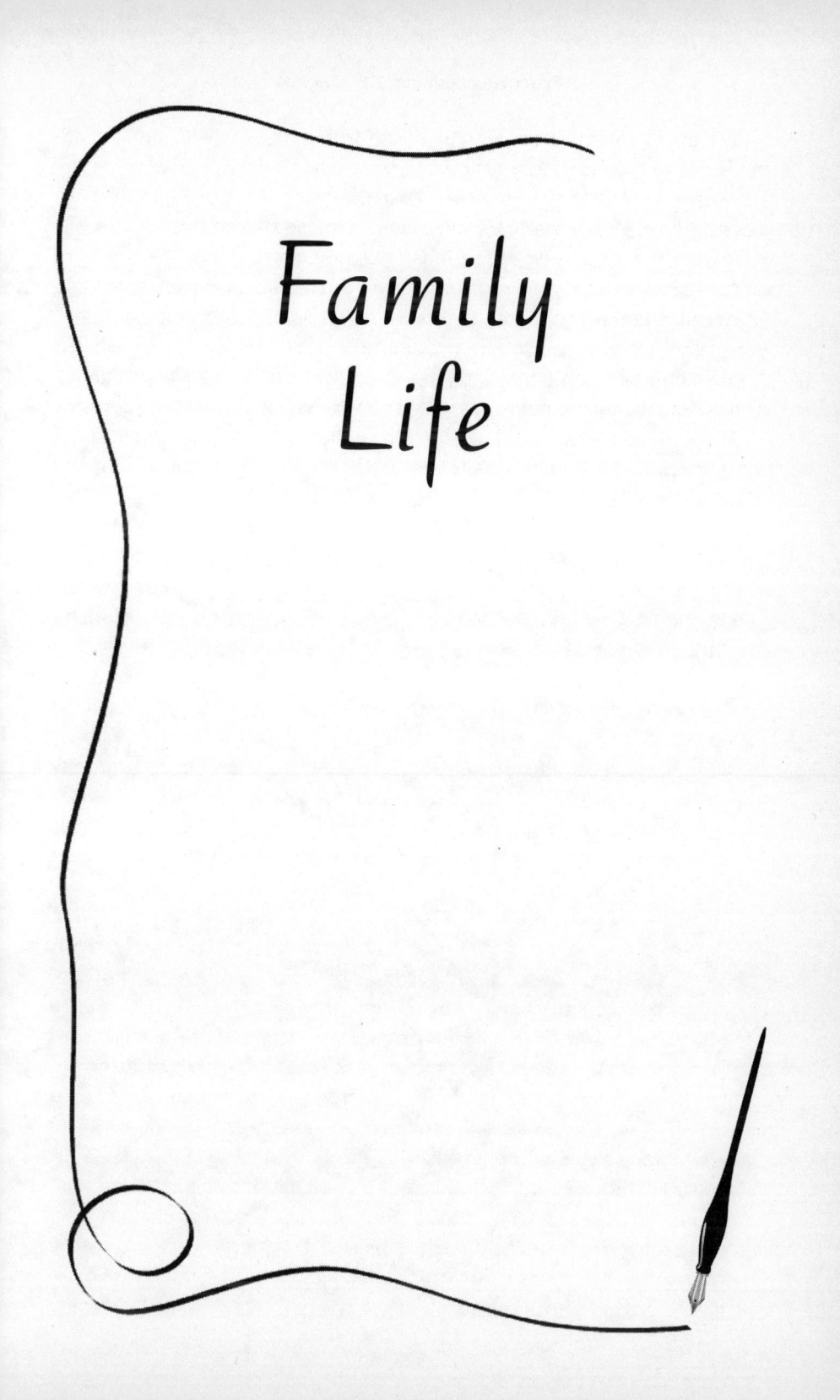

1960s
Kānga Kōpiro
~
Maringi Riddell

I love kānga kōpiro. As a child, it was my favourite dessert. I especially liked it when the kernels were minced before the cooking process, sweetened when hot, and left to set. Served cold with cream, it's delicious.

As a teenager I liked it so much I was brave enough to take some to school in a jar for my lunch. My friends would complain about the smell and not want to sit next to me. But I didn't care. They could afford to buy pies and ice cream. I couldn't. Anyway, I preferred my kānga kōpiro.

At Queen Victoria School, and later, when working as a radiographer at Auckland Hospital, my meals of kānga kōpiro became few and far between. I would crave it, but only had the chance for some when I went back to Gisborne for holidays, usually about once a year. It wasn't until I'd been married a couple of years that I decided the only way I was going to have a regular supply of kānga kōpiro was to make my own. Uncle George was the expert. He explained what we needed to do. So back to St Stephen's we went, taking with us some kernels of marigold maize. My husband Awi duly grew this, and several months later the maize was mature. The ears were carefully placed in sugar bags, tied securely, and then put into heavier sacks. Mr Jarrett, a friend of ours who ran the school farm, gave us permission to steep the maize in the nearby creek.

We had to check the bags often, especially after heavy rain. There were times, too, when a front-end loader was brought in to clean out the creek. It would scoop out our bags of maize along with the logs, watercress, etc., and dump them out onto the bank. We'd have to rescue the bags and put them back into the water. Once, one of the bags went missing. What a mystery! We thought that some of the boys must have taken it, but found no evidence to prove it. It would have been impossible for them to have cooked it without being found out. The smell would have given them away.

At the end of about four months, the maize kernels had softened adequately. The plucking, rinsing and mincing kept us busy for quite a while and, when it was done, we packed the pulp away into plastic bags and froze it.

Cooking the kānga kōpiro was a risky affair. It seemed that whenever I cooked it, that would be the time people would want to visit. I clearly remember the afternoon when my children burst in through the door after school as I was cooking some. It was their first experience of kānga kōpiro being cooked. It was amusing to see their facial expressions. They began sniffing, screwing up their faces, and then, while holding their noses, asked, 'Yuck, Mum, what are you cooking?' When I told them what it was, the rude comments began.

'Gosh it stinks.'

'How can you eat that rotten stuff?' and so on.

I turned the element off, put the pot aside, and gave them a lecture that they never ever forgot. From then on, if they found me cooking 'the dreaded pudding' as they called it, they would take a deep breath and disappear quickly down the passageway to their bedrooms, shutting the doors firmly behind them. And there they'd stay until the coast was clear.

Another time, Audrey, the farmer's wife, popped in to see me as I was cooking up a potful. I suppose you could describe her as an earthy-but-nice sort of woman. But we found her insensitive comments difficult to ignore on this occasion.

'Pooh! Your home smells like a pigsty . . . ' and 'Gosh, you Māoris will eat anything.' And it didn't stop there either. We came very close to sending her on her way and asking her not to darken our doorstep again, but we knew it was a rather minor reason for ruining a neighbourly friendship.

On another occasion, my sister-in-law, Kay, and her family came to visit. I decided to cook up some kānga kōpiro for a treat. I was quite surprised when she said that she had never eaten it before. 'Then this will be an experience for you,' I said as I served her some.

She hesitated as she was about to taste it, 'I don't like the smell.'

I looked at her encouragingly. 'Come on, down the hatch,' I said as I tucked into my plateful.

She swallowed her spoonful and then looked around at us, puzzled. After a moment of careful thought, she announced, 'It tastes like sugar bag.' We all roared with laughter.

'Is that so?' I queried. 'I haven't tasted sugar bag before.'

All this writing about kānga kōpiro has made me hungry for some. I'm going to have to be brave and have a cook-up soon. I hope my new neighbours don't come over.

1980s
Sooty

~

Oho Kaa

As we approached home with our headlights full on, a sleek black cat scampered off into the darkness. We had tried to befriend the wild thing for several nights now, but she kept her distance. We piled from the car and went straight to the bowl we had put out for her and much to our delight found she had sampled the food.

'Good,' smiled Nanna. 'When you all go back to Wellington that cat will be my friend. I shall call her Sooty.'

And sure enough, next time we visited Sooty was inside, very much at home. In fact she had produced three cuddly balls of fur and continued to do so each year. She was a very clean cat, and never ever jumped on to the table to take food. She always slept on Nanna's bed and would nudge her gently with her nose when she wanted to be let out. Whenever Nanna went away for a few days she would talk to Sooty: 'Take care of our house, now. I'll see you when I get back.' Then she would shuffle to the roadside with Sooty following her. Sooty would sit and watch until the bus had disappeared from sight then turn slowly back to the house and its surroundings.

Then one day Nanna became quite ill and went to hospital. A few days later she passed away peacefully. We discussed Sooty.

'She will be okay,' we said to our children. 'She was wild once, let her go.'

What a hue and cry that brought. 'You can't mean that. How would you like to be abandoned, especially after just losing Nanna?'

If looks could kill, we would have been dead ducks. Our two teenage daughters were heading back to Wellington that very day and, after much discussion, it was decided that Sooty would be flown to Wellington and they would pick her up at the airport. A couple of days later the rest of us were ready to travel back. We needed to get Sooty to Gisborne airport and so a cat box was hired. She didn't like the cat box at all and preferred to snuggle down on our knees for the two hour drive. At the airport a yowling Sooty was placed in the cat box and whisked away to the counter to board a plane for Wellington.

Our teenage daughters were at the other end to meet her. When they enquired about a cat from Gisborne, the air attendant said, 'Oh, *that* one,' and she disappeared. She came back with the cat box on the end of her outstretched arms, her face twisted up and her nose twitching.

'Take her quickly,' she said, 'she smells so.'

Poor Sooty, the trip must have been a real frightening experience for her. However, the girls gave her a good shampoo and soon she was out, staking her territory—and woe betide any cat that dared to come within her boundary. The children insisted that a cat door should be put in for Sooty to come and go as she pleased.

Whenever we as a family needed to return to the coast for reunions or other such functions, Sooty always flew, although we don't know if she ever got used to it. When she was seventeen human years old we discovered that she had a bad cough, and paid many visits to the vet. To relieve her, the vet prescribed some powder that was given to horses when they had colds and this certainly did ease Sooty's illness. Inevitably the day came when she could hardly walk up the stairs and finally she passed away. She sleeps now in her own patch beneath a beautiful daphne.

1950s
Greytown Hospital

~

Rachelle Calkoen

Mathijs was seven and Michiel was eight when we arrived in Waiorongomai, and we stayed there till they were ten and eleven.

They had quite a good time on the farm, as there were lots of children to play with and lots of things to do and see. On certain days, Allan, the butcher on the farm, would slaughter the sheep above the little stream near the cookhouse, and the blood and guts would attract the eels, some of them as thick as your arm. They were quite tame, which meant that they weren't slippery and you could lift them out of the water and pet them. A big attraction!

The boys would race around on their bikes or hide at the side of the road and leave a parcel or a purse on a string in the middle of the road. Cars would stop and drivers get out to see if they had found a fortune, but the moment they went to grab it, the boys would pull the string and whisk the purse or the parcel away. Good fun! And then there was the swimming pool, just for the workers and their families. The boss had his own swimming pool near the homestead. 'Our' swimming pool was quite big and just opposite the cookhouse. What a godsend in the summer!

One day Mike and Thijs were playing some cops and robbers game, when barefooted Thijs stepped on a sharp branch, which stabbed his foot. We pulled out the splinter, bandaged his foot and didn't think more about it. When Jan and I went to bed and looked into the boys' room, Thijs was obviously sick. He had a high temperature.

We rang the doctor. He lived in Featherston, about fifteen miles away. By the time Doctor Roberts arrived, Thijs was delirious.

'Blood poisoning,' was the verdict. 'I want you to take him immediately to Greytown Hospital.'

It was a very small hospital, about ten miles on the other side of Featherston, and it was past midnight when we arrived. They put Thijs in a small room just left from the front door and, as we couldn't do anything for him, we left him there and arranged to come and see him the next day at two in the afternoon.

On the dot of two, we walked into the hospital, opened the door to the little room and found . . . an empty bed, neatly made up. It was obvious that nobody had used that bed. We asked a nurse in the corridor if she could tell us where Mathijs Calkoen was.

'Who?' she asked.

'Mathijs Calkoen.'

'Never heard of him. Ask Sister, she's just coming.'

We asked the sister, who looked at us blankly.

'Who? . . . No, he's not in this hospital.'

We were starting to feel quite worried.

'But we brought him here last night, at midnight. He was in that little room.'

She shook her head. 'What's his first name?'

'Mathijs.'

'No, I've just been in the children's ward, and I'm sure there is nobody by that name.'

'But there must be!' I started to doubt whether we had taken Thijs to this hospital. The nearest hospital to Greytown was Masterton. No, no we didn't go all the way to Masterton.

'He must be here!' I repeated—and my voice started to sound shrill and hysterical.

She tried to pacify me. 'Why don't you go and see Matron?'

Off we went to the matron's office. And . . . yes, you guessed it: she had never heard of Mathijs Calkoen. We were at our wits' end when her face suddenly lit up and she said: 'Oh, you mean Charley.'

'No, Mathijs!'

'Come with me,' she laughed and we walked behind her to the children's ward. Above each bed was a card attached to the wall, on which the child's name was written in bold letters. There was: TOM, PETER, JOHN and CHARLEY. Underneath that last card was the laughing face of Thijs. 'Darling, what happened? Why Charley?'

'Oh well,' said our practical son. 'They wanted to write my name on a card, but they couldn't spell it. I tried three times to spell it for them, but they couldn't believe it, so in the end I said: "Just call me Charley!"'

1950s
Florence and Some Others
~
Shirley Dobbs Signal

Class of '52. We trainees were a cowed and driven lot. I don't know what things are like now, but in those days it was 'Them' and 'Us', 'Them' being the senior staff, most of whom had apparently never been nurses in training themselves.

If it was necessary to address a senior staff member, and one tried very hard not to have to do so, one had to stand to attention, hands behind back (why, I wonder?) and wait until acknowledged. The junior nurse was the lowest of the low. Hers was not a voice in the scheme of things. Hers but to do or die—and never, never question why!

Nursing as a career did not seem to exert much universal pull, young *Doctor Kildare* notwithstanding. There were not many of us. We had to work fairly briskly. Except in one of the three emergencies— Fire, Flood or Haemorrhage—nurses were not permitted to run. We learned very quickly to run legally by putting our heels down first. Tricky, but an essential skill to acquire.

The downtrodden junior's responsibilities extended over the entire ward. Bedpans and bedbaths were her job. She admitted all patients, stowing away clothing and valuables. She cleared away after discharged patients, and prepared the empty place for a new customer—we were never short of those. The junior nurse laid out anyone who had died, she assisted people in the shower or bath, she changed and cleaned up the bedding and clothing of those who had been unable to contain themselves (washing everything so it could be sent to the laundry), she made and cleared away morning tea for the nursing staff, and she answered every bell that rang.

If she had the misfortune to be assigned to one of the many wards without curtains around the beds, she lumped heavy screens back and forth. She fielded abuse, handled complaints, and comforted those who were afraid. When she finally came off duty, if she chanced to be working in a ward that was not quite so busy, she went to the aid of those of her friends who were still snowed under and who were likely to be an hour late coming off duty.

Eventually she would stumble into her own room, fall on the bed, ease her shoes off her throbbing feet, light a cigarette, and relax with her friends, either laughing, grumbling or weeping, depending on her emotional makeup and the events of her day. All the same, what we were doing mattered. There wasn't too much time for wondering 'What's It All About, Alfie?'—although if someone were to assume we were in the job because of altruistic motives, we would blush crimson, make some nervous joke, and run for the nearest cover.

Nine years after graduation and marriage, I was back on my old stamping ground, admitted as a patient with acute appendicitis. After the operation my doctor came to see me with the cheering news that my younger son had developed German measles. And I was six weeks pregnant! Life was somewhat fraught for the next day or so. I can still clearly see the horse syringe full of Gamma Globulin with which they skewered me, and in no time flat!

There was, however, a very powerful distraction to take my mind off things: the nursing staff and their daily routine. I have tried never to be one of those who shake their heads and say sourly, 'Ah, in my day it was never like this . . . ' But it wasn't!

For starters, there were three nurses and two trained staff on each shift. In 'My Day' we had two nurses and one trained staff, with every so often a worker on divided shift to help. Just to rub salt into the wound, a junior nurse came wandering into my room one day to see if I had any oranges she could turn into juice for me—she didn't have anything to do! Full marks to her for trying to keep herself occupied, but I nearly emptied the fruit over her head all the same!

And the equipment! Just about everything had become disposable and expendable, and therefore did not have to be cleaned and reassembled. And all the treatment trays were prepared at a central dressing station for the whole hospital. What did the nurses do with themselves all day? Well, it turned out that they still did the things that nurses have always done. They still cleaned people up, and made them comfortable, and reassured them, and contributed in large measure to their recovery.

Doctors diagnose, and institute treatments, but it's the nursing staff, in the main, who carry those treatments out: Florence, and all those others down the years, all the ladies with their lamps, or torches in this modern era. Where would the doctors be without them, let alone the patients?

Florence, you may rest easy. The lamps are still burning!

1950s
Making Scones
~
Rachelle Calkoen

We arrived in New Zealand on a Saturday. My cooking job and my husband's fencing work would start on the next Monday. We were a bit apprehensive about it all, because I could not cook and Jan had never done any fencing.

My third baby was going to be born in four weeks' time, so I rang the maternity home to book a bed.

'Who is your doctor?' asked the woman answering the phone.

'I haven't got one,' I replied. 'I've just arrived in this country.'

'Oh, but you have to have a doctor. Would you like to have Dr Roberts or Dr Frazer?'

So I rang Dr Roberts and made an appointment for Wednesday. He didn't have the time to see me earlier; this was rather awkward as my baby decided to be born on Sunday.

The boss asked my husband whether he could cook for the shepherds and the shearers, who were expected the next day, and Jan, always convinced that he can do anything, said, 'Of course!'

'Nothing special,' said the boss. 'Just the normal cooked breakfast, scones for morning tea, hot lunch, scones or simple cakes for afternoon smoko and a good cooked dinner.'

Now the difficulty was that scones don't exist in Holland, so Jan had not the slightest idea what they looked like. But he made them, with the help of three cookery books, which all said something slightly different and all three omitted to give the size.

When Jan came to visit me, at night, in the maternity home, he got out of his pocket four square, marble-sized things, which he proudly showed to me, saying; 'Look, I made some scones.'

I tried to eat one and nearly broke a tooth on it. They were as hard as a brick.

'Are you sure this is a scone?' I asked. 'Did the shearers like them?'

'Well, I suppose so. I sent a tin full to the shearing shed and it came back empty. I made enough for the whole week, six tins full!'

Some three months later the shepherds told us what happened. They looked in the tin and thought: 'This must be a Dutch delicacy.' Then they tried to eat them and couldn't, so they threw some to the dogs, who sniffed them and didn't eat them either. They ended up pelting each other with them. But they never complained. Nor did they complain about the strange meals Jan prepared for them.

They all thought: 'When the cook comes out of hospital, we'll eat well again!' Unfortunately, they were in for a nasty surprise.

1960s
Bilingual Aotearoa
~
Oho Kaa

For years my husband and I had taught in schools where English was the only language, the sole Māori input being the odd action song or haka. Then in the late 1960s we won a position at a four teacher school in the Bay of Islands—Matawaia. The community's first language was Māori but it had been forbidden in the school.

Matawaia. What fond memories that name brings. It was a rural community situated eight miles inland from Moerewa. One needed to look hard to see the sparsely dotted homes amongst the trees, swamp and scrub. The drains, or creeks, as they called them, were almost level with the road, making it prone to flooding.

My husband had to drive our Zephyr slowly, as the stones on the road were rather large and there were lots of them, too. We had never encountered a roadway such as this before. We did not see any sign of a township, but we caught up with a young lad on horseback and enquired as to where the school might be.

Without looking at us he pointed up the road, and said, 'Or dare.'

Thank you, we smiled and continued our drive.

Then suddenly there on a rise stood a green painted four classroomed school. I was so glad to see how high up we were. I couldn't bear the thought of being flooded out. So this was Matawaia school, our new challenge. There was just the headmaster's house, on a rise behind the school and surrounded by fruit trees galore, and to the right another house for the assistant teacher.

Our five children jumped out, eager to explore our new surroundings. We found out very quickly that the school was the hub of the community. Once a week the doctor would come and use the staff room for his consulting room and the patients would sit outside on the forms waiting to be called. Sometimes the doctor would have to come into the classrooms to find his patients. We all paid the equivalent of 50 cents a visit.

The dental nurse also came in periodically and set herself up in a section of the staff room. She would stay just until she had attended to all the pupils' teeth. Sometimes this was two weeks, other times it was three.

My husband came home chuckling after meeting his school committee for the first time. The chairman opened the meeting in Māori and then translated what he had said for the benefit of the new principal. As each member of the committee spoke, the chairman would rise to translate their speeches. Then my husband was invited to say a few words.

He stood up slowly, cleared his throat and proceeded in Māori to thank the group for their warm welcome. He continued, telling them what he would hope to achieve while we were there. By this time the committee members were shuffling in their chairs, and surprised exclamations of 'Wii' and 'Aue!' were heard. The atmosphere during the tea break that followed was hilarious: the laughing, chattering and the shaking of heads in disbelief. But it sealed the acceptance of a person from another tribal area.

Another incident happened with the children themselves. A deputation came in to see my husband.

'Please Sir, may we speak Māori at school?'

He stopped what he was doing, looked at the deputation and replied, 'If you want to speak Māori then it must be good Māori, just as is required when you speak English.'

I have never in my life heard so much cheering and yelling. The children's faces were just radiant. Word spread like wild fire throughout the whole school. For a while this posed a slight discomfort for me. I had to run up to the other end of the school to find out what some of the words that the children were using meant. Here were these five-year-olds speaking Māori flat tack.

One day I came across one little girl crying her eyes out in the cloakroom. 'What's the matter, Marcia?' The sobbing continued.

'I can't help you, dear, if you won't tell me.' Sobbing continued.

My husband passed by and I explained the situation to him. He simply said, 'Speak to her in Māori.'

Again I turned to Marcia.

'He aha te raruraru, Marcia?' ('What's the trouble, Marcia?')

The answer was instant. 'Aku hū, kua ngaro aku hū.' ('My shoes, I've lost my shoes.')

These experiences and many others have committed me to do all I can to help bring about a bilingual Aotearoa.

1980s
Topsy
~
Maringi Riddell

When Topsy was born she was probably just like any other piglet—pink, cute, and hungry. She would have been about three months old when Awi bought her, along with another weaner, to fatten up for bacon and pork.

Right from the beginning her behaviour could be described as most 'unpiggylike'. She fell hook, line and sinker for Awi the moment she saw him. You could say it was love at first bite. Instead of being frightened of him when he approached with buckets of food, she'd walk up to him, flop down in front of him, and beg to be scratched. She'd follow him at every opportunity, and she loved to rub up against him.

As the months passed by, she endeared herself to her lord and master so much that, when it came time to kill her, he just couldn't do it. And so, after many years of buying weaners, fattening them up and killing them, Awi decided that Topsy would have to stay, and that he would breed his own pigs.

Awi called her Topsy because she was particularly fond of Topsies, a food she ate fairly regularly when the school freezers broke down, or when there were long powercuts.

When it came to the time to take her to the boar for mating, she would obediently climb up onto the tractor tray and be taken to the neighbouring farm. On arrival she would get off and be left to the mercy of the boar. Awi didn't like leaving her there because the other sows would attack her. They were probably jealous of her because she was much better looking than they were. Luckily she was more than a match for them physically, and was able to look after herself. After a day or two away, she was eager to be collected and brought back home.

The birth of her first litter was a memorable experience. We watched her closely as her time neared, and she rose to the occasion. The day beforehand, she began gathering heaps of straw and lily leaves, and made a huge nest. Then, when everything was to her satisfaction, she lay down on her bed and waited.

It was a sleepless night for Awi. Peter, a neighbour, came over with a bottle of whiskey, and together they kept Topsy company. By the grey morning light, they counted seventeen little piglets, the biggest litter she was ever to have. She was a wonderful mother—always even-tempered and trusting, allowing Awi to handle her babies whenever he wanted to.

A year or so later, Topsy developed a large abscess on her neck. With Awi holding her, she allowed the vet to lance the abscess and pull out the many lumps of pus, standing quietly all the while. The vet was most impressed.

Over the years Topsy provided many litters of healthy piglets. She was a much loved pet. When she became too old, Awi couldn't bring himself to put her down, so he decided to send her off to the works. It was a very sad time for all of us to see her disappear down the drive. She went so willingly, we felt we had betrayed her. Poor dear, she probably ended up as sausage meat.

Awi chose a successor from one of Topsy's piglets. This potential mother had a lovely long body, just perfect for the job (so he thought). Unfortunately, her attitude and temperament didn't match her body. She was nasty and uncooperative. It was impossible to get her to do anything, or go anywhere. It was a miracle that the boar managed to get her pregnant.

After her first litter, she became even more nasty, attacking anyone who came near her. When she chased Tania, who was heavily pregnant at the time with Mahaki, forcing her to fall as she scrambled over the fence to safety, Awi decided she would have to go. (The sow, of course, not Tania.) So, as soon as her litter was weaned, she got the bullet. And that was the end of our pig-breeding days.

1970s
Night Sights
~
Lesley Ferguson

It was peaceful watering the back garden at night. A time to think. A time to let the day's cares wash away. But Ian was distracted from his thoughts by a strange disturbance behind the boy's lighted window. Something had fluttered out of sight. He dropped the hose and stepped across the dripping broccoli for a clearer view.

He could see the Bilbo poster, and the dragon one, on the wall above Richard's bed. The model aircraft suspended from the ceiling wobbled in turbulence. A faint moaning could be heard.

Now he picked his way over the lettuces. The sprinkler, disregarded, turned on him and drenched head and shoulders. Ian stole closer, and now a ladder was visible inside. A ladder? A white sheet-covered figure was climbing up to the top to plummet down and bounce on the bed. It arose, threw back its hood and danced devilishly before the night-darkened reflective window.

As Ian watched, the wizard Gandalf raised his arms slowly, drew back his lips and stretched his mouth wider with hooked forefingers. A fierce tongue was thrust out and the wizard admired his scary reflection; then nearly fell with fright when, with a crunch of gravel path, a terrible face appeared from the dark, pressed against the glass— a flattened nose, dripping hair, fanged grin. Ian's bellow of laughter matched the boy's squeal of embarrassment, and the watering and dreaming came to an end for that night.

1970s
Camping at Waikawa
~
Maringi Riddell

In the summer of 1972, after borrowing a caravan to go camping at Cape Runaway, Awi and I decided to buy our own. And so, before the next summer, we had ourselves a brand-new caravan—matching awning, gas refrigerator, camp toilet, plus all the lightweight gear to go with it.

Our children, Mark, France and Tania, were aged thirteen, twelve and eight at the time, and we had planned to spend our holiday at Waikawa, which is approximately twelve miles from Te Kaha, in the Bay of Plenty. It was to be a real family affair. About five other families from our whānau would be there, and we'd been lucky enough to secure a camp site on McDonald's farm, under the pohutukawa trees, close to the beach. Our plan was to join the others after Christmas Day.

On Boxing Day we started packing in earnest, and soon realised that the task was bigger than we'd realised. We had made up a checklist-cum-camping recipe book, and expected to be ready to go in a couple of hours. It wasn't that easy. Four or five hours later the excitement had disappeared, and tempers were beginning to flare. Then began the 'verbal exchanges'. The trip was nearly abandoned, due to the impatience of one stressed-out Dad who had planned to get away early so that there'd be plenty of time at the other end to set up camp before dark. Quite justified, too, but I didn't think it was all my fault that we were going to be late.

Our children were caught up in the middle of it all, trying hard to be helpful, but getting the hard word too. We (the kids and I) had a quick conference and decided that perhaps Dad could go by himself and we'd stay home. But no—we knew that we really did want to go. I was left wondering whether 'getting away from it all' was worth all this trouble.

Eventually we set off with our Valiant and caravan bulging at the seams. Tania, the youngest, who was sandwiched between Mark and France, was complaining bitterly. 'I never get to sit next to the window. Why do I always have to sit in the middle? We should have turns by the window,' and so on. And of course, every twenty minutes or so, the inevitable question, 'Are we nearly there?' Oh dear! It was going to take us every bit of seven hours to get to Waikawa. However, as the journey unfolded, the atmosphere warmed up. We were soon 'on speaks' again, and ready for the great outdoors.

We arrived at Waikawa to a warm welcome. Setting up camp was exciting and soon done, with everyone helping. Later, after a meal, we were grateful to be able to collapse into bed. You would have thought a good night's sleep was in order, but in the wee small hours of the morning the farm rooster put an end to that. If I could have caught the damned thing I would have gladly killed it.

Camping for a long period of time can be great fun if it's fine, and not so great if it's raining. However, we'd thought to bring along lots of indoor games for the kids to play (Monopoly was a favourite) and a stack of books.

We organised our jobs so that no one member, Mum in particular, had to do too much housework. We had also decided that each person had to do their own washing, which meant going down to the creek armed with Cold Water Surf, a bar of Taniwha soap, a big plastic washtub, the clothes of course, and plenty of energy. Our clothesline was made up of a long length of rope strung up in the pohutukawa branches.

Camp cooking was a pleasant task. Most of the cooking was done over the open fire. We had special black pots for this, a camp oven and a kettle that whistled when it boiled. Only if it was really wet would we cook indoors on the gas stove. We tried to conserve our gas to keep the refrigerator going. On hot days, it was sheer luxury to have cold drinks.

Carefree days were spent swimming, reading, sunbathing, playing cricket, walking and, when the tide was out, collecting seafood—paua and kina mainly. Mark was very skilful with his Hawaiian sling and kept us supplied with fish. For the first couple of weeks or so, we gorged ourselves on fish and seafood. We would cook it in as many different ways as possible: battered, smoked, curried, raw, boiled, pan fried, you name it, we did it. After a while, though, we started craving meat. Then we'd pull out a couple of tins of corned beef, and cook it up with onions. Served with freshly baked camp bread, it was delicious. Even the humble sausage proved to be a much appreciated treat.

New Year's Day was a memorable occasion. A hāngi was the order of the day, and we all joined in with the work. The children collected the wood, the women prepared the vegetables and desserts, and the men tended to the meat and seafood. What a hākari—delicious hāngi food served with such delicacies as crayfish mornay, marinated mussels, paua fritters, salads of all descriptions, followed by corn pudding, fruit salad and such. The wonderful togetherness, the goodwill, and the beautiful setting, all added up to a magic moment in our lives.

The days passed by quickly, and all too soon it was time to pack up and go home. The thought of it brought another sort of excitement: the longing to get home, to have a decent bath, to sleep in comfortable beds, to wash clothes in a washing machine, to watch TV, and so on—everyday luxuries we take for granted.

Driving through the Bombay Hills was always an exciting part of the journey home, and by the time we pulled up outside our house, the children would be ecstatic. They would burst through the door and run through the rooms calling out, 'Hello home! Hello home!'

There's nothing quite like a long camping holiday to make you appreciate your own home.

1960s
The Basket Social
~
Oho Kaa

Fundraising for the Matawaia school took many forms. It was always a community effort, with much preparation beforehand. There were the usual gala days, calf clubs, pet shows, fancy dress balls, concerts, bring and buys and cake stalls, but the one that I remember so well was the basket social.

The school committee had decided that they would have a basket social and we the teachers would be welcome to come along and be part of the evening. Each class was expected to put on an item or two for the parents.

'What is a basket social?' I asked.

'Oh you just make up a basket of food and take it down for supper.'

I pondered over this in between getting the children to practise their play and songs over and over again until satisfied that they would be able to do it with their eyes closed.

For the next few weeks the room was a hive of industry—me bustling around with paper, glue, paint, materials, wool and scissors, and the children ever eager to create their own costumes.

Then finally the day arrived. The excited children, including our five, had been sent home early that afternoon supposedly to rest before the big event.

That evening, there was very little prompting from us. In no time at all our family were dressed in their long pants and skirts. With our basket of cakes and sandwiches tucked into the boot and all the children's bits and pieces for their items, we were soon wending our way down to the hall.

The place was already astir, sweet strains of 'Pokarekare Ana' drifting out from the hall. Up on the small stage was the local band of talented teenage boys, looking so well groomed in their best strides. A few youngsters sat along the edge of the stage, eyes glued to the band.

One could almost hear them saying, 'I want to be able to do that too, one day.'

We made our way to the supper room, greeted cheerfully by children and parents alike, but we were somewhat surprised to note that ours was the only box in the supper room. We walked back into the hall to be greeted by the chairman who told us how the evening would proceed.

With the help of the senior children and our junior assistant, we soon had all the costumes into the tiny changing rooms on each side of the stage. The children performed superbly, uninhibited by the crowd watching them. The chairman thanked them for their wonderful efforts. Then it was on to the next on the agenda: the bidding for the baskets. As each family name was called, a huge box requiring two people to lift it was brought forth from under their seats and carried on to the stage.

The chairman announced that the bidding for each box would start at a dollar. The first basket went for four dollars. By the fourth basket we thought we would put in a bid. At that time the bidding was at five dollars. Our bid took it to ten. The chairman raised his hands for another bid, but not a sound was heard. My husband, to applause from the hall, duly paid and took our newly acquired basket into the boot of our car.

As there were still a few boxes to go, my husband said he may as well take our basket home so that the boot would be empty to cart all the costumes and things back to school later. Meanwhile, the bidding continued, until all the baskets were sold.

Then came the real surprise. Supper time.

Each family gathered round their basket and waited patiently while each huge linen tablecloth was spread out on the floor. This took up most of the floor space round the hall. Then all the food was laid out—stuffed pork, roast chicken, smoked eels, kumara still piping hot wrapped in foil, potatoes, various salads, heaps of cartwheel bread, delicious steamed pudding, fresh cream, bowls of fruit salad, bananas, chocolate biscuits, mixed lollies, cordial and soft drinks, and even paper plates, paper bowls, paper cups and plastic knives, forks and spoons. It was a real feast. Our children had been claimed by their friends to eat with them, as were others who were left standing around.

Can you imagine how we felt? We were making our way to the car to bring back the basket when the chairman, sensing our embarrassment, came out and assured us that no way were we to bring back that basket we had paid for. The family who brought it would be offended. In fact they thought it was an honour for the teacher to bid for their basket. I wasn't totally convinced, but we came back into the hall. Everyone was tucking in heartily yet still took time out to offer us food. From the supper room came our sandwich and cake box, which we placed on the tablecloth. To our delight, both were quickly snatched by enthusiastic little hands.

1990s
Middlemore
~
Lesley Ferguson

The Wednesday morning is just right. Stuart is showered, lying back relaxed. Morning sun is pouring into the ward, and conversation is flowing. Vegetarian talk; holistic medicine; and Mr Kong sitting cross-legged ready to meditate. Mr Boroski is positively making a point about riding his bicycle again—'and I vill,' he says. He is eighty-four, and the other patients' conversation only occasionally penetrates his hearing.

Into the ward stroll the Important Four: the trim-suited specialist, two nurses and a young doctor. It has been difficult to find a doctor to consult with, so far, but the nurses and cleaning lady have been helpful! After days of anxiety and curiosity, here is my opportunity to hear informed opinion. How is it progressing? Will he keep the foot? Why is the wound still oozing, and so angry?

'Good morning.' A nod of the well-groomed head to Stuart, whose wild thatch for once looks soft and silky, in contrast to his newly developed goatee stubble. Murmurings from The Four as the swollen foot and lacerations are inspected.

'Ice packs?' Yes.

'Movement?' Some forwards, back and a little sideways movement, of course.

'Hmmmm.' Not looking at us. Not a word of explanation—or comfort.

'Another fortnight here. Keep all weight off it.'

'Oh.' I try not to show dismay. Stuart's face clamps up, his expreszsion nearly undoing me. I stand up and seek the view from the window, my back to the world.

The team has switched their attention elsewhere. The elderly

Lithuanian is demonstrating his two well-mended hips—but 'No more bicycles, though.' The Eminent Four leave the ward without a backward glance.

Two weeks! How will he bear it in this ward with no family, few friends and no cycling, running or parapenting prospects—and, I thought, who would do his washing?

'Come on, Mum,' says Stuart, also trying to hide his disappointment.

'You know,' says an Asian voice, 'it's only another fortnight. The nurse here says she has been trying to get out for 20 years!'

Mr Kong lifts his double-pinned hand to a more comfortable position.

Stuart has two crutches, two feet and has advertised the parapent and hang-glider for sale.

Thoughtfully trying to cheer me up, he muses, 'You know, if I had died I'd be happy with my life. I've had some wonderful times, and though I'll not be parapenting or hang-gliding again, I'll still be able to get some great dives.'

1980s
Houseboat Holiday
~
Mavis Boyd

'This should last for a week,' said Gilbert as he heaved an enormous block of ice into the ice chest on the deck of our houseboat.

We were making a family visit one lovely autumn, and my brother had thought of a way in which we could all be together on neutral territory. By renting a ten-berth houseboat on the River Murray in South Australia we achieved at one stroke a solution to the questions of sleeping accommodation, entertainment, shared activity, shared leisure, and individual needs for privacy.

Each one brought produce from farm or garden. There were grapes, purple and green, baskets of oranges, buckets of tomatoes, bulging lettuces, home-killed meat, eggs from Doris's hens and deep green pumpkins. When a week's supply of food for a large family is assembled, it is a spectacular sight.

Although the galley was well equipped, Gilbert brought his large portable barbecue along, so that not only was he captain of the ship but chief cook as well, a role his wife and sisters were happy to relinquish.

The weather was delightful. The days had the lingering warmth of late summer touched with the clarity and stillness of autumn. Our vessel, utilitarian rather than elegant, chugged along at four knots. This stately pace matched the gentle drift of the river. After breakfast we could sit in comfortable chairs on the deck while one person steered the boat and kept a watchful eye out for hidden logs and other dangers.

Binoculars gave close-up views of pelicans, black swans or other nesting birds. Swallows constantly formed an unpaid guard of honour. Did they rest, I wondered? Were they the same swallows or did they accompany our boat a little way and then drop off to be replaced by others? Did they feel, as we did, an identification with this temporary floating home? At sunset, the boat would be moored to comply with river laws. In the morning there were often birds on the rail, waiting to take up escort duty again.

Occasionally we met another houseboat, and then the quiet air would ring with the sounding of horns and calling of friendly greetings. There was a momentary fragile bond of kinship with these strangers, based solely on the fact that they had chosen the same form of transport as we had.

After lunch we would go ashore and walk in the long grass and bracken, the air scented by eucalypts. We might pass a tree, its trunk white, its branches covered with pink galahs, clustered like thick blossom—extraordinarily beautiful to passers-by, menacing to farmers.

In the evenings we would play Scrabble, five hundred and the games of our childhood. Once again we were a family in our own little world, coming together in this brief bubble of time.

At times we would leave the games with their easy laughter and exchanges and go outside in the dark. We stood together in the mild fragrant air, silenced by the beauty and intensity of the close stars.

Each evening when the boat was moored my nephew put out the fishing lines and sometimes there was a treat, a whole fish for each person, crumbed and cooked to perfection by Margaret. So the days passed in easy, languorous succession.

Going downstream, and again on our return, we had to pass through a lock. People who are used to river life know all the courtesies and rituals connected with this procedure: the sounding of the horn to announce one's approach and alert the lock-keeper, and then the respectful waiting at a suitable distance while he emerges, bluff and genial, from his comfortable house to operate the lock.

How startling it was to find a house surrounded by trees—carefully selected trees, not gums—beds of flowers and a bright green jewel-like lawn of manicured perfection, an oasis in the monotonous beauty of cliff, dried grass and gum trees. Had I dreamed the lock-keeper's house? No. On our return journey there it was again, startlingly incongruous.

Sometimes a flock of birds flew overhead, wheeling in mid-flight as to an unseen command. What mysterious force held them together in such unity that they turned as one?

One day a family of Aborigines was sitting on the bank. We waved. They waved. Then their hands drooped and they sat quite still, utterly motionless, silently gazing at us until we moved out of their range.

Walking one day we disturbed a kangaroo who did not desire our company. He began to lope away and then, coming to a fence, soared easily and gracefully into the air with his great bulk, disappearing among the gum trees.

On the last morning there was a scurrying to pack our belongings. Suddenly thoughts turned to families and homes, children and grandchildren. There was wiping out of ovens and refrigerator. Gilbert wiped out the ice chest, discarding the block of ice, now pathetically small.

Cars were waiting at the houseboat terminal. We said our goodbyes. So much said. So much unsaid.

1960s
Jinty
~
Rachelle Calkoen

There was such a big age difference between our youngest son and the two older ones that we thought it might be a good idea to contact Social Welfare, to see if they needed a temporary home for a three- to five-year-old child, either male or female.

They thanked us enthusiastically and that was it. We didn't hear from them until two years later, when we got a telephone call: could we please have a girl for the weekend? Her mother had run away to the South Island, her father wanted to go to find her and Social Welfare didn't like the idea of the girl all by herself, at home.

'How old is she?' we asked.

'Fifteen years old. She works, and will come to your house on Friday straight after work, if you agree.' We agreed.

I asked Thijs if he minded vacating his room for this girl, and Mike didn't mind having Thijs in his room for the weekend. We shifted some beds, made Thijs' room look welcoming and waited for Jeannet to arrive. When she hadn't arrived at 5.30 p.m., I began to worry and rang Social Welfare.

'Don't worry,' they said, 'she'll be there.'

At 10 o'clock at night she still hadn't come. I rang a Social Welfare officer I knew and got the same answer: 'Don't worry, it is not your responsibility.'

We went to bed with the nice feeling that we could sleep in the next morning. Flip, who was four and a half, had other ideas about that. He was a very active child and always tried to trick us out of bed, with things like: 'Dad, there is a telephone call for you,' or 'Somebody is knocking at the door.'

This Saturday was no exception. 'Mam, there is a lady at the door.'

'Oh yes, ask her to come in.' He ran back to the kitchen door and we thought, yes, he's a good actor. But we were a little astonished to hear high heels clicking on the kitchen floor. I shot out of bed, threw on a dressing gown and met a lady in the hall. She had an enormous teased hairdo and a thickly painted face, which looked, scowling, at me. It suddenly dawned on me that she must be Jeannet. And I was right.

'We expected you last night,' I said.

'Yes . . . well, I couldn't find the house, so I stayed with my boyfriend. As a matter of fact I wasn't sure if this was the house, so I left the taxi waiting down below, with my luggage.'

We lived on a bushy hill, 150 steps up from the road. It was a beautiful spot, with sun all day and lovely views over the bay, but you couldn't see the street from the house so I took pity on her and asked Mike and Thijs to go down to help her bring her luggage up.

I wasn't prepared for the amount of things they came back with: two suitcases and two cardboard boxes, one full of gramophone records and one full of make-up. I had never seen so much make-up in my life. There was hardly room to put it all on the lowboy in Thijs' room, and there was no way all her clothes could fit in his wardrobe.

She installed herself, came out of the room and asked if we had a gramophone, and then proceeded to dance to her collection of pop records, all by herself in our large and sparsely furnished sitting room.

Our big boys, eleven and twelve, were absolutely fascinated. They thought Jeannet was just fabulous! We weren't so thrilled, especially when I asked her, on Sunday night, what time she had to be at work on Monday.

'Oh, I'm not going to work on Monday. I've got to be in the hospital at 9.30.'

'Why?' I asked.

'Oh, you know, a routine VD test.'

I went to see Jan to ask if a VD test was what I thought it was, and we thought that Social Welfare should have given us a bit more information about this girl that we had taken into our family.

Her father hadn't come back by Monday so Jeannet stayed and I asked what time I had to wake her for work.

'I'm not going to work on Tuesday. I'll have to be in Court at ten.'

'What for?'

'Well, my boyfriend is up for a charge of carnal knowledge and I'll be there, so they can see that he couldn't know I was under age.'

All this came out in a calm and matter-of-fact way. I just stood there with flapping ears. In 1962, not only did you not talk about this subject, you certainly would not admit to sexual intercourse when you were only fifteen!

I never went to bed before Jeannet was home and we often sat together drinking coffee and smoking cigarettes till late at night.

One evening she said: 'You should call me Jinty, all my friends do!'

She told me about her experiences at home and in the borstals and institutions she had been sent to at different times, and we got quite fond of each other, which was lucky, because she stayed with us for over three months! Her father never came back and Social Welfare didn't find a suitable place for her, but in the end, we felt it was not fair to ask Thijs to vacate his room for a weekend and lose it for three months. So we started hassling Social Welfare.

But Jinty did not want to leave. She loved living with us. She felt at home because, she said, 'I'm not accepted in society and neither are you, because you are only bloody foreigners, that's why we get on so well. Both outcasts!' We laughed about that, but maybe there was some truth in it . . .?

One nice episode while Jinty was with us happened on Mother's Day. Our family never took much notice of Mother's Day, so I knew it was Jinty's present when I came into the kitchen and found on the bench two square cake tins filled with earth, little shells all around the edges and lovely cacti and succulents inside. As a joke, I said: 'Oh Jinty, where did you steal those lovely arrangements?'

She answered quite earnestly, 'From the third house to the left, up the road.'

1980s
Top Four
~
Maringi Riddell

Watching World Cup Rugby finals brings it all back—the suspense, the excitement, the pain of losing, the ecstasy of winning. We have been there and done that, my husband and I. He, as the coach of the Te Aute College First XV, and I, as the manager.

The year, 1984. We had won the right to represent the Central Regions district in the quest for the top First XV in the country. St Stephen's School, Bombay, was the other North Island team, and the two South Island teams were St Bede's and Otago Boys' High School. Christchurch was the venue for the tournament, and our departure date was set for Wednesday, 8th August, with the finals to be played on Saturday, 11th.

Thursday night we came up against St Bede's. The hard, close-fought encounter was played under lights in extremely cold and windy conditions. After an excellent start, with the wind favouring us, we built up a handy lead. But this was whittled away gradually by St Bede's in the second half, and we just managed to scrape in with a 21–16 win. In the other encounter, St Stephen's won comfortably against Otago Boys'.

This meant that we would meet St Stephen's in the final. It would be our second encounter for the season as we'd already played them in June during our annual traditional fixture. They had thumped us 22–3 on their ground, leaving us stunned. There was nothing we could do to counter their brilliant play that day, and so it was 'back to the drawing board'. We were thrilled to get a second chance to play them, and this time we were better prepared.

On the Friday before the final game, Tane Norton came and spoke to our team. What a wonderful speaker and motivator he was. In his quiet, assertive manner he told the boys to put the earlier defeat out of their minds. This was to be a different ball game on neutral ground. He talked about attitude, concentration, commitment, and supportive play. We were enthralled by his address—you could have heard a pin drop.

Saturday, the day of the final, was fine but windy again. The scene was set for a cracker of a game. Rugby Park was crowded, and Tom

Doocey, the top New Zealand referee at the time, was to control the game.

We won the toss, and our captain decided to follow Tane Norton's advice and take the kick. The blast of the whistle began a game that had everything one could wish for: atmosphere, drama, excitement, skill, dedication, hard running, and no quarter given by either side. As the game progressed we had the feeling that St Stephen's was a little over-confident, and somewhat surprised that our team was matching them in the forward play, an area that they had dominated in our earlier encounter. However, with the wind at their backs, they scored first—a try that was unconverted.

Gradually our forwards began to dominate the lineout and scrums and, from a pushover, our halfback, Terence Hokianga, scored. This try also was unconverted, and so at half-time the score was tied at 4-all.

In the second half, with the advantage of the wind, we felt confident. Things seemed to be going our way. The crowd too seemed to favour us. Perhaps it was because we were the underdogs, or that we sported the same colours as the Canterbury team, red and black.

Although we had the edge over St Stephen's, we couldn't break their defence, and so our second five-eighths, Hallam Kupa, decided to strike out with his boot. He landed a drop kick from about forty metres out, making the score 7-4. We screamed and danced with delight, but the joy was short-lived. St Stephen's came back at us stronger than ever, and almost scored again. Luckily their Number 8 was brought down by magnificent tackling, and the ball was short of the line.

Those last few minutes were agonising, with both teams trying desperately to gain dominance. And then, in a huge wave of supportive play, our halfback scored again. I nearly collapsed with the tremendous excitement of it all. But no! The try was disallowed—unsighted by the referee. Oh the pain! It was the St Stephen's supporters' turn to breathe a sigh of relief. The winning of the game was still within their reach.

And on the game went. Would it never end? Five minutes to go, and it seemed an eternity. At last the final whistle sounded with our boys still trying valiantly to get over the line. There were scenes of utter joy, and utter despair. It was our turn to rejoice. We were the victors this time. We had turned the tables on them and won the big one, 7-4.

After the presentation we all crowded into the changing room, and someone produced a bottle of celebration bubbly. The cup was filled and passed to players and supporters alike. Tom Doocey came to congratulate Awi on a great game, and walked into the shower to congratulate our captain, Te Maari Tikao.

Later, at the aftermatch function, much to everyone's amusement, Wes Burns, a member of the St Stephen's Board of Governors, and an old friend of ours, got down on his hands and knees and kissed Awi's shoes, saying, 'You bugger! I knew you'd be too clever for us. I told them to watch out for you.'

The remainder of the trip was all a wonderful blur. It was weeks before we came down from cloud nine and back to reality.

A couple of years later, Tom Doocey announced his retirement. We felt deeply honoured when he singled out this Top Four final as the most exciting and memorable game he had controlled in his career as an international referee. Praise indeed from a man with a reputation such as his.

I still get a warm fuzzy feeling when I think about it all.

1950s
Meeting the WDFF

Rachelle Calkoen

The Women's Division of Federated Farmers was something I knew absolutely nothing about and, having come from Amsterdam where there are no farmers, I wasn't very interested. But here is this stern-looking female who has stepped into my kitchen and demanded my attendance at the meeting of the WDFF that evening.

I had just come to the cookhouse with my new baby; I had the worry of cooking for the shepherds, and was very concerned about my seven- and eight-year-olds, who had to travel fifteen miles to the nearest school. I was very tired and explained to my visitor that I really didn't think WDFF would be something for me. Doris lived in one of the cottages on the other side of the paddock and was adamant. 'The last cook never went, and the ladies were quite offended about that. If you want to start off on a good footing, you'd better go. I'll come and collect you at 7.15.' I was really terrified of her and promised I would be ready.

She was there on the dot and in the car explained to me that WDFF was great fun: they had competitions in cake baking, sewing and flower growing and often had a speaker on interesting subjects such as millinery, flower arranging, cake decorating and so on. My heart sank.

We were welcomed by the president, an ample woman in a pink frock who introduced me to the members as the new cook of Waiorongomai. I had to stand up for a round of applause. After the business part of the meeting was over, Delia—the pink lady—suggested that I judge the flowers. Every member had brought three different flowers: one single bloom, one cluster and a third category which now escapes me. There were so many flowers that I had never seen in my life before, like birds of paradise, protea, bottlebrush, leucodendron etc. I was absolutely fascinated and I gave the prizes for all the wrong reasons to all the wrong people.

While we were having a cup of tea, some ladies came up to me and said, 'So, you're the new cook. Could you please give us some cooking hints?'

Whereupon I replied, 'Oh no, I'm no good at all, you will probably be much better at cooking than I am.'

Another one said: 'Would you like some knitting patterns for your new baby?'

'Well no, I can't knit.'

Somebody tried: 'Then you must be a good gardener.'

'No, really not. We used to have a gardener at home and we weren't allowed to touch the garden.'

That did it. If you can't talk about recipes, knitting patterns or gardening, what is there left to talk about? They abandoned me, and I stood there feeling miserable and useless.

After the tea break, somebody spoke about origami, and then Delia asked if anybody had any suggestions for a speaker for the following meeting. Nobody reacted.

I stood up. 'Couldn't you get a doctor to talk about family planning?'

Doris, who sat next to me, pulled me hastily down on my chair. Delia was very red in the face, and you could cut the silence in the hall with a knife.

Delia coughed a few times and then said: 'Any other suggestions? No? Then I declare the meeting closed.'

Doris steered me with a firm hand to the exit. In the car, she collapsed with laughter, 'Oh Rachelle,' she said, 'I really think the WDFF is not for you.'

It was eighteen years later that Dr Roberts spoke to them about family planning!

The Authors

Joyce Harrison grew up in Wellington where she and her husband now live. She has an MA (English) and Diploma of Social Science from Victoria University, and has been a teacher, social worker and social research worker. She enjoys flute playing, poetry, reading, bridge and family activities.

Heather Williams was born in 1928, and in the course of growing up lived in Palmerston North, Ashhurst, Invercargill and Wanganui. In 1947 she married Lance Williams and has lived in Wellington since then. She and Lance have four children and twelve grandchildren. She has been active in a number of community groups, local choirs and the Porcelain Artists' Association. Her recreations include sailing, tramping, porcelain painting, gardening, tennis and badminton.

Rachelle Aleida Calkoen was born in Amsterdam, Holland, in 1923. She trained in Child Psychology and migrated to Australia in 1954, moving to New Zealand in 1958. She has three sons and six grandchildren and enjoys spinning, embroidery, rug making, reading and classical music.

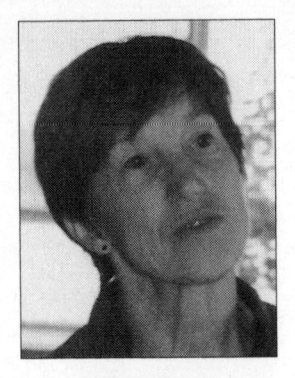

Lesley Ferguson lives at Paraparaumu with her husband, a retired pilot. She is a Wellingtonian, born and bred. After Queen Margaret College she studied at Massey Agricultural College (as it was then) for her Horticultural Diploma. She has two sons and loves family life, art, reading, writing and her garden.

Oho Kaa was born at the Waipiro Bay Maternity Hospital on the East Coast of Aotearoa. After three years at St Joseph's Māori Girls' College and two years at Wellington Teachers' College she returned to the East Coast to teach at Rangitukia. She is married with a family of three boys, two girls, and six grandchildren. She has been an itinerant teacher of Māori language, co-ordinator of the Ngata Dictionary and an editor with School Publications. She currently works with Huia Publications.

Jeannette Hunter was born in Amsterdam, Holland, in 1921. After the war she became a Montessori kindergarten teacher. After marrying an Australian she emigrated to New Zealand in 1961. She taught in Petone and Eastbourne primary schools from 1968 to 1984. She has two sons and two grandchildren. Now retired and living in Otaki, she pursues her hobbies—swimming, spinning, weaving, music and reading.

The Authors

Kay Carter was born in Cambridge and spent her childhood on a farm at Monavale. She attended Waikato Diocesan and Hamilton Technical College. After working for Federated Farmers and the New Zealand Post Office she married at eighteen and now has four children and six grandsons. She has lived in various parts of New Zealand and overseas. Her first husband died in 1978 and she remarried in 1982. Retirement in 1993 presented new challenges, including making some order from her accumulated letters, albums and diaries.

Maringi Riddell of Iwi Te Aitanga-a-Mahaki, Hapu Te Whanau-a-Taupara, was born in Gisborne in 1940. After attending Queen Victoria School she worked as a radiographer and a teacher in Auckland, Hawke's Bay and Petone. She is currently an editor (Māori) with Learning Media. She is married to Te Aorere and has three grown-up children.

Shirley Dobbs Signal was born, in 1928, into a tumultuous period in New Zealand's history—the Great Depression and World War II. After college she embarked on a musical career overseas as a pianist, but returned home to train as a nurse, and marry. After fourteen years of marriage, two sons, a daughter and divorce, she returned to music, teaching at home and in schools for 23 years, enjoying every moment of it. Now retired, she lives in Raumati.

Mavis Boyd grew up in vineyard country—the Barossa Valley of South Australia. She came to New Zealand in 1957 to train as a teacher and graduated with a BA in English and German. She has two daughters, three stepsons and three grandchildren. Now retired, she lives in Khandallah, Wellington, where she enjoys playing the flute, gardening, walking and reading.